Facilitator's Guide

A GUIDE TO
CO-TEACHING

SECOND EDITION

A Multimedia Kit for Professional Development

A GUIDE TO
CO-TEACHING

Practical Tips for Facilitating Student Learning

SECOND EDITION

RICHARD A. VILLA

JACQUELINE S. THOUSAND

ANN I. NEVIN

A Joint Publication

CORWIN PRESS
A SAGE Company
Thousand Oaks, CA 91320

Council for
Exceptional
Children

For information:

Corwin Press
A SAGE Company
2455 Teller Road
Thousand Oaks, California 91320
www.corwinpress.com

SAGE Ltd.
1 Oliver's Yard
55 City Road
London EC1Y 1SP
United Kingdom

SAGE India Pvt. Ltd.
B 1/I 1 Mohan Cooperative
   Industrial Area
Mathura Road, New Delhi 110 044
India

SAGE Asia-Pacific Pte. Ltd.
33 Pekin Street #02-01
Far East Square
Singapore 048763

Printed in the United States of America

ISBN 978-1-4129-5487-7

This book is printed on acid-free paper.

08 09 10 11˙ 12 10 9 8 7 6 5 4 3 2 1

Acquisitions Editor:	Allyson P. Sharp
Editorial Assistant:	David Andrew Gray
Production Editor:	Eric Garner
Copy Editor:	Paula L. Fleming
Typesetter:	C&M Digitals (P) Ltd.
Proofreader:	Charlotte J. Waisner
Cover Designer:	Michael Dubowe

Contents

About the Authors

Richard Villa, Jacqueline Thousand,
and Ann Nevin.
Working, Learning, and Teaching Together!

 Richard A. Villa, EdD, has worked with thousands of teachers and administrators throughout North America. In addition, Rich has provided technical assistance to the U.S., Canadian, Vietnamese, Laotian, British, and Honduran Departments of Education. His primary field of expertise is the development of administrative and instructional support systems for educating all students within general education settings. Rich has been a middle school and high school classroom teacher, special educator, special education coordinator, pupil personal services director, and director of instructional services. He has co-authored and co-edited nine books and authored over 100 articles and book chapters regarding inclusive education, differentiated instruction, collaborative planning and teaching, and school restructuring. Known for his enthusiastic, knowledgeable, and humorous style of teaching, Rich is a gifted communicator who has the conceptual, technical, and interpersonal skills to facilitate change in education. His professional development activities include short-term keynote addresses and papers presented at national and international conferences, two-day guided practice workshops for school teams, three-week intensive workshops, three-to-five day programs, and semester-long (15 weeks) programs offered through universities.

 **Jacqueline S. Thousand,** PhD, is a professor in the College of Education at California State University–San Marcos, where she co-coordinates the special education professional preparation and master's programs. Prior to living in California, she directed the Inclusion Facilitator and Early Childhood Special Education graduate and postgraduate professional preparation programs at the University of Vermont. While there, she also coordinated several federal grants, all concerned with providing professional development for

educators to facilitate the inclusion of students with disabilities in local schools. Jacqueline is a nationally known teacher, author, systems change consultant, and advocate for disability rights and inclusive education. She has authored numerous books, research articles, and chapters on issues related to inclusive schooling, organizational change, differentiated instruction and universal design, cooperative group learning, creative problem solving, and co-teaching and collaborative planning. She is actively involved in local school reform initiatives in the San Diego area, most recently assisting elementary, middle, and high schools in establishing co-teaching and Response to Intervention (RTI) approaches to provide all students access to the core curriculum and early intervention supports. She also is actively involved in international teacher education endeavors and serves on the editorial boards of several national and international journals. Jacqueline is a versatile communicator who is known for her creative, fun-filled, action-oriented teaching style.

 **Ann I. Nevin,** PhD, is professor emerita, Arizona State University, and visiting professor, Florida International University. The author of books, research articles, and numerous chapters, Ann is recognized for her scholarship and dedication to providing meaningful, practice-oriented, research-based strategies for teachers to integrate students with special learning needs. Since the 1970s, she has codeveloped various innovative teacher education programs, including the *Vermont Consulting Teacher Program* (a Bureau for Education of the Handicapped U.S. Department of Education–funded grant award), *Collaborative Consultation Project Re-Tool* (sponsored by the Council for Exceptional Children [CEC, 2003]), the Arizona State University program for special educators to infuse self-determination skills throughout the curriculum, and the Urban Special Education Academic Leaders (SEALS) doctoral program at Florida International University (an Office of Special Education and Rehabilitative Services U.S. Department of Education–funded grant award). Her advocacy, research, and teaching spans more than 35 years of working with a diverse array of people to help students with disabilities succeed in normal school environments. Ann is known for action-oriented presentations, workshops, and classes that are designed to meet the individual needs of participants by encouraging introspection and personal discovery for optimal learning.

Introduction

We designed this guide to accompany the study of the book, *A Guide to Co-Teaching: Practical Tips for Facilitating Student Learning*, 2nd edition, by Richard Villa, Jacqueline Thousand, and Ann Nevin, along with the video/DVD *Co-Teaching* by Richard Villa, Jacqueline Thousand, Ann Nevin, and Carl Harris. We offer a framework to assist facilitators involved in professional development and course instructors who prepare teachers at the preservice or in-service levels.

Based on our experience in giving and receiving staff development, we can attest to the importance of programs that provide ongoing support for teachers, especially when they are learning innovative practices. We agree with Giordano (2005), who found that teachers are more likely to change their teaching behaviors when the professional development program is grounded in practice, intellectually stimulating, collaborative, and sustained over time. She concluded,

> The teacher is the gatekeeper of change in the classroom, and staff development designed to change teacher practice must be guided by and integrated with teachers' existing values, valences, knowledge, and behaviors. Changing values and beliefs along with well-established behaviors takes time. (Giordano, p. 52)

For these reasons, we use four principles to guide our differentiation of instruction for the activities, applications, and discussion questions described in this Facilitator Guide.

First, we use *multiple methods* of providing access to the content to be learned and informally assessing the impact of professional development through observation of participants as they engage in various workshop activities. We summarize each of the chapters in our book, as well as provide sample discussion starters, workshop and video/DVD activities, and ideas for application to participants' classrooms.

Second, we tap *multiple levels of cognitive development* by providing a variety of discussion questions to guide the reading of the book to prepare you, the facilitator, for successfully leading a study of both the book and the video/DVD. By encouraging participants to discuss how they can create and evaluate their own co-teaching applications, the discussion questions go beyond the knowing and understanding levels. As shown in Figure 1, the questions reflect the newest understandings of cognitive development (according to a revised taxonomy of learning objectives by Anderson & Krathwohl, 2001).

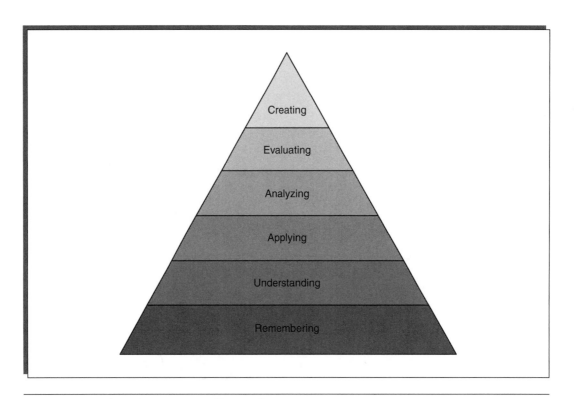

Figure 1   Bloom's Taxonomy (Revised)

Note the changes from nouns (e.g., "the application level") to verbs (e.g., "applying"). Schultz (2005) notes the change in positioning of the previous evaluation level, now described as "evaluating," from the top of the taxonomy to the second tier, while the previous synthesis level, now described as "creating," has moved to the top. In addition, this Facilitator Guide encourages individuals to tutor (self- or peer-) or study with others in a small group in which members read and discuss the content of the book and the video/DVD segments. This provides an active learning forum for people to compare and contrast their emerging understanding of the concepts.

Third, we *differentiate options* that facilitate either your own learning or the learning of others. The goal is that, as a facilitator, you can provide a model of the differentiated strategies that you want the teachers to practice with their pupils. You may choose to facilitate independent study, small study groups, workshops, or an entire university course. You can vary how participants access content about co-teaching by reading the text, viewing the video/DVD segments, reflecting upon and discussing content or observations, or visiting classrooms to observe practices in action.

Fourth, we *empower teachers to meet nationally recognized sets of standards* specified for novice teachers, either the Interstate New Teacher Assessment and Support Consortium standards (INTASC, 2006) or the Council for Exceptional Children standards (CEC, 2003) for beginning special educators and, for veteran teachers, the National Board for Professional Teaching Standards (NBPTS, 2006). All of these standards include competencies related to collaboration with others to differentiate instruction to increase student achievement.

For independent study, participants may follow the six steps listed below to study the contents of each chapter:

1. Read the assigned chapter in the book and check unfamiliar terms by reading the Glossary.
2. Review the handouts/overheads as an introduction to the video/DVD segment(s).
3. Watch the corresponding video/DVD segment(s).
4. Reflect on the discussion questions.
5. Complete the practical application(s) for chapters, when available.
6. Find colleagues who are implementing co-teaching approaches, talk to them about the practices featured in the chapter, and ask to observe their instruction.

For small study groups using the book, participants can do the following:

1. Read the assigned chapter in the book in advance, using the Glossary to learn unfamiliar terms, and bring one or two questions, important learning outcomes, or examples from their own classrooms to share with the group.
2. Rotate the role of group facilitator among study group members. At assigned meetings, the facilitator guides members through the following steps:
   Step 1. Review the concept map found at the beginning of each chapter as an introduction to the chapter content and video/DVD segment(s).
   Step 2. Watch the corresponding video/DVD segment(s).

Step 3. Take turns answering discussion questions with group members.

Step 4. Take part in one or more of the activities suggested for a workshop.

Step 5. Complete the practical application(s) for chapters, where available. If participants are expected to apply strategies between sessions, time will need to be built into the subsequent session for debriefing and sharing experiences.

Step 6. Invite a study group partner to co-plan a lesson using one or more of the co-teaching approaches.

Step 7. Observe peers who are co-teaching or set up a peer coaching experience with one or more study group partners who are using the co-teaching approaches.

For a small or large group workshop, the facilitator(s) can guide the participants to complete the following steps:

1. Review the concept map found at the beginning of each chapter as an introduction to the chapter content and video/DVD segment(s).
2. View the corresponding video/DVD segment(s).
3. Answer the discussion questions.
4. Complete the practical application(s) following the workshop, then return for the next session prepared to share what happened. An alternative is to arrange to e-mail the facilitator, and perhaps one or two others, a paragraph summarizing what happened.
5. Use the Glossary to help learn terms that may be unfamiliar. Copies of the Glossary should be distributed to participants.
6. Share one or two questions, important learning outcomes, or examples from the classroom. Be sure to allow time in the workshop for this step.

For a workshop series, the facilitator(s) can do the following:

1. Review the concept map found at the beginning of each chapter as an introduction to the chapter content and video/DVD segment(s).
2. Show the corresponding video/DVD segment(s).
3. Ask participants to answer the discussion questions.
4. Invite small groups to demonstrate one or more of the activities.
5. Ask participants to complete the practical application(s). If participants are expected to engage in applications between workshops, time will need to be built into the subsequent workshops for debriefing and sharing of experiences.

6. Ask participants to implement the strategies and co-teaching lesson plan components learned to that point with students back in their classrooms. Facilitators may arrange for observation and coaching of participants implementing the lessons. If participants are expected to apply strategies between sessions, facilitators will need to allow time for debriefing and sharing in the subsequent workshop.

7. Distribute copies of the Glossary to each participant without a book to help in the learning of terms that may be unfamiliar. If participants have the book, ask them to read assigned chapters before the next meeting and check for unfamiliar terms in the Glossary. They should then bring one or two questions, important learning outcomes, or examples from their own experiences to share with the group.

8. Structure time in each session for questions and sharing of important learning outcomes or examples from participants' own classrooms.

For undergraduate or graduate courses, instructors can lead the class with these steps:

1. Develop a syllabus of class sessions that reflects both the expected content and the objectives of the course, as well as discussion questions and applications identified for each of the chapters in the book.

2. Have class participants read assigned chapters in the book before upcoming class meetings, checking for unfamiliar terms in the Glossary. Participants should bring one or two questions, important learning outcomes, or examples from their own experiences to share with the class.

3. Complete the video/DVD activities in each class so that participants can observe actual classroom examples.

4. Assign the discussion questions provided in this Facilitator Guide as in-class activities and/or as homework assignments for guiding participants to digest the content of each chapter.

5. Use the applications suggested for each chapter as a form of performance assessment, allowing course participants to show their competence in using the principles and strategies introduced. Instructors should differentiate the applications based on the years of experience as teachers (e.g., novice teachers, such as student teachers or first-year teachers, may want to meet INTASC standards, while veteran teachers may want to meet NBPTS) and include applications that may correspond to requirements for credentialing programs or undergraduate and graduate degree programs.

6. Structure time for participants to share one or two questions, important learning outcomes, or examples from participants' own classrooms.

How to Use the Video/DVD

The video/DVD is designed as a springboard for discussion for all 12 chapters of the book. The Epilogue does not have a corresponding segment on the video/DVD. As support material to illustrate concepts discussed by the authors of the book, *A Guide to Co-Teaching: Practical Tips to Facilitate Student Learning,* 2nd edition, the video/DVD is directed toward administrators, teachers, staff developers, instructional coaches, curriculum coordinators, preservice and graduate education teacher preparation faculty, educational consultants, parents, school district members, and other leaders in K–12 schools. The video/DVD (the content of the video and the DVD is identical) can help both facilitators and participants visualize how these techniques are applied in a classroom setting.

The video/DVD menus are clearly titled to correspond to chapters in the book, and the activities using the video/DVD are denoted in the Contents for easy reference. The video/DVD includes footage of actual co-teaching lessons at the elementary, middle, and high school levels as well as comments from teachers, students, and administrators.

What Facilitators Should Know About Practical Applications

We recommend that participants apply what they are learning in the book in their classroom settings. The best applications are useful for either novice or veteran teachers. For example, there are *make and take* activities, in which teachers generate lesson plans and take them home to implement; *model and demonstrate* activities, in which teachers observe a lesson and then analyze the successful elements in preparation for their own demonstrations; *coax and coach* activities, in which experienced teachers observe lessons and provide encouragement as well as substantive corrective feedback; and *listen and learn* activities, in which the facilitator can lecture using a lecture guide.

We encourage staff development personnel and facilitators to be aware of and sensitive to the need for adequate time to digest information, reflect and engage in meta-cognitive thinking, practice new skills, and celebrate as participants move through the stages of development from novice to veteran co-teachers. We remember that accommodations must be made for teachers who are at different stages of development in their professional expertise. These differences influence both willingness and ability to co-teach. Also, we remember that it takes time to achieve mastery of a complex teaching repertoire such as co-teaching. For these reasons, we designed the Practical Applications in accordance with the National Staff Development Council (NSDC) recommendation that, once initial knowledge about a new instructional practice has been provided, follow-up application activities should reflect the best practices (Roy, 2005) shown in Table 1. We like to say, "Learning to co-teach is a journey, not a destination!"

What Facilitators Should Know About Relevant Standards From Professional Organizations That Govern Teacher Certification

What are the skills, knowledge bases, and dispositions that co-teachers need to meet the seemingly competing mandates of the No Child Left Behind Act and Individuals with Disabilities Education Improvement Act? Two studies were conducted independently (Cramer & Nevin, 2006; Liston, 2006) in elementary and secondary classrooms. In two urban, metropolitan, multicultural school districts (Miami and San Diego), general and special educators working as co-teachers were observed and interviewed through surveys and interviews. As reported by Cramer, Nevin, Thousand, and Liston (2006), when co-teachers engage in collaborative planning and teaching, they are demonstrating standards (shown in Table 2) related to at least three different professional teaching organizations—the Interstate New Teacher Assessment and Support Consortium (INTASC) standards for beginning general and special educators, the Council for Exceptional Children (CEC) standards for beginning special educators, or the National Board for Professional Teaching Standards (NBPTS) for veteran teachers at all levels. The co-teachers were clear about why they wanted to co-teach: "We want to meet the academic and social needs of different learners in our classrooms."

Meeting professional standards can be an important source of motivation for teachers. Co-teaching allows teachers to demonstrate standards related to how learners are different, how to use a variety of instructional strategies, and how to collaborate and communicate with people from other professional viewpoints. Both novice and veteran teachers benefit when co-teaching

Table 1 Professional Development Best Practices Associated With Practical Applications

Best Practice	1	2	3	4	5	6	7	8	9	10	11	12	Epilogue
Observe a co-teaching lesson and listen as the teachers debrief the lesson.				*	*	*	*	*	*				
Arrange an observation and debriefing of a co-teaching lesson with a master teacher.							*						
Read an article about one or more of the four co-teaching approaches and discuss it with others.				*	*	*	*	*					
Review sample co-teaching lesson plans and adapt them for your students.				*									
Co-plan and co-teach lessons with a coach or knowledgeable peer.		*									*		
Plan with a study group to implement one or more of the four approaches to co-teaching.		*	*	*		*	*				*		
Videotape one of your co-teaching lessons and request feedback from a peer, coach, or administrator.							*						
Problem-solve issues that arise when you implement co-teaching in your classroom.		*						*	*	*	*		*
Assess your level of implementation of co-teaching. (Use *Are We Really a Co-Teaching Team?*)											*		*

Note: The authors developed the activities for this guide to reflect the best practices identified in an essay by P. Roy in the February 2005 National Staff Development Council (NSDC) Newsletter.

professional development activities are related to teacher certification standards. Meeting standards such as those described in Table 2 is one way in which all teachers can feel more competent that they can help all their students master the general education curriculum. Perhaps most importantly, facilitators who use this Facilitator Guide can emphasize that participants will gain skills to build and maintain collaborative relationships and instructional strategies to guarantee more effective co-teacher interactions. This means that co-teachers gain not only instructional strategies but a whole set of planning and collaborative skills, as well as approaches to co-teaching that can be connected to the standards and, by implication, to the credentialing programs for each state.

Table 2   Analysis of the Professional Standards That Co-Teachers Demonstrate

Classroom Teachers INTASC (2006)	Special Educators CEC (2003)	Experienced Teachers NBPTS (2006)
Standard 3 requires teachers to understand *how learners differ.*	Knowledge and skills in understanding characteristics of learners with *different cognitive, physical, cultural, social, and emotional needs*	Teachers adjust their practice according to *individual differences in their students.*
Standard 4 requires teachers to *use a variety of instructional strategies.*	Competencies related to *knowledge and skills for instructional content and practice*	Teachers show *multiple methods* to engage student learning and to enable students to reach goals.
Standard 10 asks teachers to *collaborate and communicate* with parents, families, and colleagues to support student learning.	Competencies related to *communication and collaborative* partnerships	Teachers *collaboratively work with others* and coordinate services.

Additional Resources and Tips for Facilitators

Corwin Press offers a free, 16-page resource titled *Tips for Facilitators* that describes different professional development opportunities, the principles of effective professional development, the characteristics of an effective facilitator, the responsibilities of the facilitator, and practical tips and strategies to make a meeting more successful. *Tips for Facilitators* is available free of

charge as a download at the Corwin Press Web site, www
.corwinpress.com, under "Extras." We recommend that facilitators
examine the *Tips for Facilitators* guide and pay particular attention
to the characteristics and responsibilities of facilitators and the professional development strategies for different types of work groups
and settings.

Welcome and Workshop Starter

● *Welcome Activity #1. Workshop Introduction Activity*

Time: 10–15 minutes
Directions:

1. Welcome the participants and thank them for giving you their time and attention.
2. Introduce yourself and note your background related to co-teaching.
3. Poll participants about their various roles (administrator, general education teacher, special educator, paraprofessional, related services personnel such as speech and language consultant, etc.).
4. Poll participants about the age level of the students they serve (early education, elementary, middle level, secondary, university, etc.).
5. Poll participants about their years of experience with the practice of collaborative planning and teaching on behalf of their students. For example, you can ask the following questions and have participants raise their hands:
   • Do you have one to two years of experience?
   • Do you have more than two years of experience?
   • Is this your first year?
   • Have you not co-taught yet but know that co-teaching is in your future?
6. Ask participants to identify any burning questions or issues about co-teaching that they or their colleagues want addressed. If the audience is small, you can have them call out the questions and issues as you record the items on poster paper. If the audience is large, distribute index cards and ask participants to write their questions and issues on the cards. Collect the cards to review later. Tell participants that their questions and issues will be addressed in the workshop content or during the scheduled question-and-answer period.
7. Ask "What is co-teaching?" Immediately begin Welcome Activity #2—The Cocktail Party Activity.

● *Welcome Activity #2. Cocktail Party Activity*

Time: 15 minutes
Materials:

Overhead transparency of Handout 1: Definition of Co-Teaching.

CD player or MP3 player, musical recordings stored on a computer, and speakers. Select an upbeat musical selection.

Directions:

1. Show transparency of Handout 1: Definition of Co-Teaching.
2. Tell participants that they will participate in a cooperative group learning activity referred to as the Cocktail Party.
3. **Directions for the Cocktail Party:** "When the music begins, everyone mixes by moving or dancing around the room. When the music stops, participants freeze and form a pair with the nearest person. As the facilitator, I will ask a question that both partners will answer within 45 seconds. As soon as the music begins again, begin moving or dancing around the room again until the music stops and a new question is posed. You will have four opportunities to speak with different partners. You must have four different partners. Choose a partner only when the music stops.
4. **Let the Party Begin:** The first time the music stops, ask Question #1: *"What are the benefits to you personally and professionally when you collaborate to plan or teach lessons?"* Remind them to be sure each partner has a turn to speak and that they will have no more than 45 seconds to exchange their ideas.
5. After 45 seconds, play another round of the Cocktail Party by starting the music again. When the music stops, ask Question #2: *"What effect does collaboration have on the students we teach?"*
6. Repeat for a third round, asking Question #3: *"How does adult collaboration affect the school climate?"*
7. Repeat for the final round, asking Question #4: *"What is your greatest challenge in achieving collaboration?"*
8. Finish by saying, "It's time to thank each other and say goodbye!" Ask participants to return to their seats while playing a different musical selection.
9. Debrief by sampling several responses to each of the four questions. Affirm all responses. Tell participants that the chapters they read will provide additional answers to the four questions and will assist them in dealing with the inevitable challenges of beginning a new educational innovation such as co-teaching.

Chapter-by-Chapter Study Guide

A Guide to Co-Teaching: Practical Tips for Facilitating Student Learning, Second Edition

by Richard A. Villa, Jacqueline S. Thousand, and Ann I. Nevin

Part I: Introduction to Co-Teaching

Chapter 1: What Is Co-Teaching?

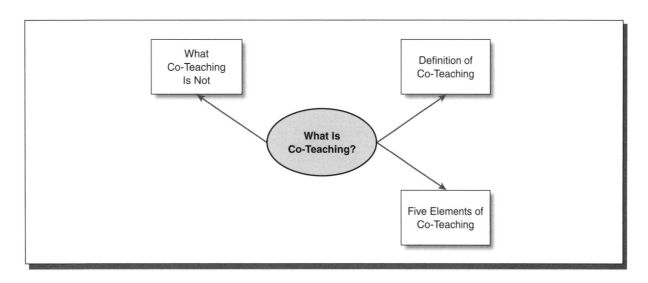

Figure 1.1   Content Map for Chapter 1

Summary

Co-teaching is two or more people sharing responsibility for teaching some or all of the students assigned to one classroom. Co-teaching is not new to education. Many teaching arrangements look like co-teaching. Many do not (e.g., one person teaching one subject, followed by another person teaching a different subject; one person teaching while another person photocopies materials; one person conducting a lesson and others watching). Co-teaching in the 21st century is one of the most innovative practices in education and is more likely to meet individual learner needs. It is a fun way for students to learn from two or more people who have different ways of thinking, it is a way to make schools more effective, and it is a creative way to connect with others to help children learn.

Co-teaching is like a marriage. Sometimes, it is a marriage of choice. Other times it is an arranged marriage, as is common in some cultures. As with all marriages, partners must learn to trust each other, communicate, be creative, and resolve conflicts.

Co-teaching includes five basic elements: (1) at least one common goal; (2) a shared belief system where each co-teacher is valued for unique expertise; (3) parity between the co-teachers who both give and receive information or advice and learn each other's skills; (4) use of a distributed functions theory of leadership, where what one teacher traditionally did is replaced with a shared distribution among all co-teaching team members; and (5) a cooperative procedure with face-to-face interaction, positive interdependence, monitoring and processing interpersonal skills, and individual accountability.

Discussion Questions

1. From your knowledge and experience so far, complete these two sentence starters. *"Co-teaching is . . ." "Co-teaching is not . . ."*
2. How do the authors define *co-teaching*? What is the advantage of explaining what co-teaching is not?
3. Do you agree or disagree with the statement, *"From a teacher's point of view, co-teaching can help teachers differentiate instruction."* Why or why not?

Practical Application

1. Create your own compare/contrast chart to help you learn the distinctions between what co-teaching is and is not.

Activities for Workshop Facilitators and Course Instructors

There are two activities that facilitators can choose to offer participants: (1) Cooperative Group Learning Jigsaw—Five Elements of the Cooperative Process and (2) Video/DVD Activity—What Co-Teaching Is and Is Not.

● *Activity #1. Cooperative Group Learning Jigsaw—Five Elements of the Cooperative Process*

Time: 10 minutes
Materials:

Handout 2: Five Elements of the Cooperative Process for Co-Teachers: Note-Taking Guide

Text:
- If participants have a copy of the text, *A Guide to Co-Teaching: Practical Tips for Facilitating Student Learning*, 2nd edition, they will read the subsections of the chapter that refer to the five elements of co-teaching.
- If participants do not have the text, photocopy the sections devoted to the five elements of co-teaching so that each group member has a different element.

Directions:

1. This is a cooperative group learning jigsaw activity. First, assign participants into teams of five.
2. If the participants have the book, assign one of the five elements described in the book to each team member of each group. If a team has fewer than five members, assign one or more of the members an additional rationale to ensure that all rationales are read by each group. If the participants do not have the book, distribute photocopies of each of the five elements so that each person in a group has a different element. The five elements include (1) at least one common goal; (2) a shared belief system where each co-teacher is valued for unique expertise; (3) parity between the co-teachers who both give and receive information or advice and learn each other's skills; (4) use of a distributed functions theory of leadership, where what one teacher traditionally did is replaced with a shared distribution among all co-teaching team members; and (5) a cooperative procedure with face-to-face interaction, positive interdependence, monitoring and processing interpersonal skills, and individual accountability.

3. Instruct the team members to read the assigned element silently and prepare to teach it to their teammates. Suggest that they create a visual representation of the content to use during their instructional time. Provide participants no more than three minutes to prepare.

4. Distribute Handout 2, the blank note-taking guide for the elements. Explain that each person on the team has one minute to share the assigned element and that Handout 2 is to be used for taking notes on each of the five elements as they are taught. There are three rotating roles during instruction. Explain the roles as follows:

   Instructor/Teller—Explains the assigned rationale to teammates.

   Questioner/Clarifier—Asks any clarifying questions to ensure complete information is shared by the instructor/teller.

   Timekeeper—Warns the instructor/teller when one minute is nearly up and signals when one minute is up.

5. The person whose birthday is closest to today (either before or after) will be the first instructor/teller. The person to the instructor/teller's right is the first questioner/clarifier. The person to the right of the questioner/clarifier is the first timekeeper. Roles rotate to the right on each subsequent round, so that the first questioner/clarifier becomes the second instructor/teller, the first timekeeper becomes the second questioner/clarifier, and the person to the right of this original timekeeper now becomes the new timekeeper for the second round. This rotation of roles continues until each team member has had a chance to teach the assigned element.

6. Ask team members to discuss their own cooperative process. Begin the discussion by having them thank one another for their instruction.

7. Close this activity by saying, "Please tell your team which one of the five elements is the most important to you as a co-teacher and why."

● *Activity #2. What Co-Teaching Is and Is Not*

Video/DVD Activity
Time: 30 minutes
Materials:

Handout 3: What Co-Teaching Is and Is Not

Video/DVD cued to the segment titled "What Is Co-Teaching?"

Laptop and/or TV monitor and video/DVD player

Directions:

1. Distribute Handout 3: What Co-Teaching Is and Is Not.
2. Before watching the video/DVD, ask participants to think about and write down, in the "Co-Teaching Is Not" column of Handout 3, non-exemplars or bad examples of co-teaching. After about a minute, ask several participants to share their non-exemplars. Then tell participants they will hear from one of the authors of the book what good co-teaching looks and sounds like.
3. Ask participants to watch, listen, and take notes as Dr. Richard Villa explains what co-teaching is as he overviews the four approaches to co-teaching.
4. Play the Video/DVD segment titled "What Is Co-Teaching?"
5. When the segment is complete, ask participants to add ideas to their copy of Handout 3: What Co-Teaching Is and Is Not.
6. After about one minute, ask one or two participants to share their notes with the whole group.

Chapter 2: Why Co-Teach? What Experience, History, Law, and Research Say

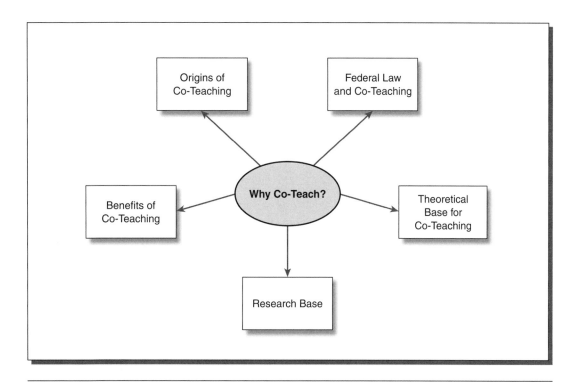

Figure 2.1   Content Map for Chapter 2

Summary

The purpose of this chapter is to expand your beliefs and attitudes about the benefits of co-teaching. First, the history and evolution of co-teaching are briefly outlined, starting with the 1960s, when co-teaching was introduced as a progressive education method, and continuing to the present, when co-teaching serves as an effective instructional arrangement for achieving federal mandates to provide all students equitable curriculum access from highly qualified teachers (e.g., the No Child Left Behind Act of 2001 and the Individuals with Disabilities Education Improvement Act of 2004).

Collaborative teaching has some background in epistemological and psychological frameworks such as Glasser's Choice Theory (1999), Johnson and Johnson's Social Psychological Theory (1989), and Vygotsky's Zone of Proximal Development (1987). What are the documented benefits of co-teaching for teachers, students, and schools? From preschool through high school, we know that students with disabilities can be educated effectively in general education environments where teachers, support personnel, and families collaborate; and students' academic and social skills improve through co-teaching.

Furthermore, co-teaching results in the following benefits for students and teachers:

- Increased flexibility
- More immediate and more accurate individualized instruction
- Increased positive attitudes toward school work
- More use of strategies that feature active learning, which leads to increased achievement
- Higher ratings of satisfaction, because co-teachers meet their own basic needs as well as the basic needs of their students
- Higher capacity to meet a variety of student needs, especially the need for belonging and the need for changes in routine that can be fun (such as listening to peers instead of teachers).

Discussion Questions

Decide what you would say in response to the following questions. You may work alone by responding in a personal journal, or you may discuss your answers with a partner or teammates in a small group.

1. Which rationale described in this chapter supports your own practices, beliefs, and feelings about the benefits of co-teaching? Are there other reasons for co-teaching? Compare

your answers with those of your colleague(s). Notice that you and your colleague(s) may find different rationales compelling for varying reasons.

2. In your opinion, why might co-teaching become easier over time?

3. What are some examples of how co-teaching could help students and teachers move from feelings of isolation to feelings of community when "the Lone Arranger Model of teaching is replaced with a Co-Teaching Model?"

Practical Applications

1. Conduct a Web-based search on the key words *co-teaching* and *team-teaching*. What do the articles or sites that you find say about co-teaching or team-teaching and their effects on students and teachers?

2. Plan a quick lesson (10 to 15 minutes in length) with a colleague in which you each have a role as co-teaching partners. After delivering the lesson, debrief by discussing what you observed regarding the students' reactions and levels of engagement, as well as your own experiences during the co-taught lesson. Did you experience a sense of belonging, empowerment, choice, or fun?

Activities for Workshop Facilitators and Course Instructors

There are two activities that facilitators can offer participants: (1) Summary and Guided Practice Jigsaw and (2) Video/DVD Activity—Why Co-Teach?

● *Activity #1. Summary and Guided Practice Jigsaw*

Purpose: The purpose of this activity is to empower participants to complete the study guide, "Why Co-Teach: Multiple Rationales."
Time: 20–30 minutes
Materials:

Overhead transparency and photocopies for participants of the content map for Chapter 2

Directions:

1. Show an overhead transparency and distribute a copy of the content map for Chapter 2. Quickly review the content of the chapter.

2. Organize the participants into three-member study groups. Tell the participants that each member of the study group will be responsible for reading, summarizing, and reporting to the study group. Assign each member of the group a letter *A, B,* or *C* where
   - *A*'s will study and teach the documented benefits of collaborative teaching for teachers, students, and schools.
   - *B*'s will study and teach the history and evolution of co-teaching.
   - *C*'s will study and teach the legislative and theoretical underpinnings.
3. Give participants about 25 minutes to complete this activity.
4. Ask the participants to thank their study group partners and quickly move on to the next activity.

● *Activity #2. Why Co-Teach?*

Video/DVD Activity
Time: 10 minutes
Materials:

Handout 4: Note-Taking Guide for Video/DVD of Chapter 2: Why Co-Teach?

Video/DVD cued to segment titled "Why Co-Teach?"

Laptop and/or TV monitor and video/DVD player

Directions:

1. Distribute Handout 4: Note-Taking Guide for Video/DVD of Chapter 2, "Why Co-Teach?"
2. Ask participants to watch and listen to the video/DVD and take notes using Handout 4: Note-Taking Guide as Dr. Richard Villa explains several rationales for co-teaching.
3. Play the video/DVD segment titled "Why Co-Teach?"
4. When the segment is complete, ask participants to take a minute to add any ideas to their copy of the note-taking guide that they had not yet noted or to add their own rationale for co-teaching.
5. If participants have copies of the book, also ask them to look at the headings and rationale statements presented in Chapter 2 to detect additional reasons for co-teaching not covered in Dr. Villa's presentation.
6. Ask participants to share the rationales they found most compelling, including any additional rationale they added to those presented by Dr. Villa.

Chapter 3: The Day-to-Day Workings of Co-Teaching Teams

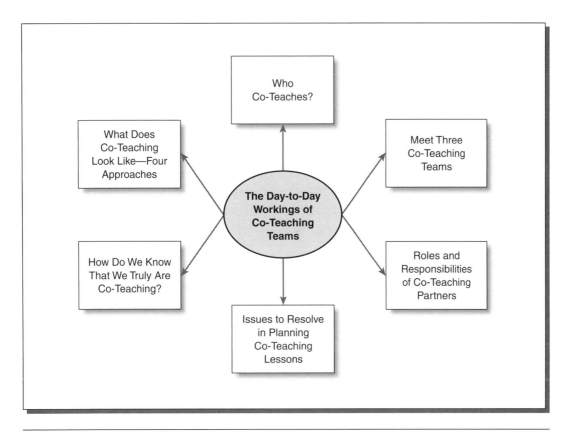

Figure 3.1   Content Map for Chapter 3

Summary

In this chapter, participants are introduced to a variety of people who might be co-teachers. Members of three co-teaching teams are introduced to illustrate the many faces of co-teaching. Next, four approaches to co-teaching are briefly described (supportive, parallel, complementary, and team-teaching) through word-pictures of what co-teaching might look like in action. The roles and responsibilities of co-teachers are outlined for before, during, and after lessons as well as the organizational, logistical, instructional, and communication issues that must be resolved. Co-teachers are encouraged to self-assess as they acquire and practice the multiple dimensions of effective co-teaching.

Discussion Questions

Answer the questions, either working alone and writing your responses in a personal journal or working with a partner or small group and discussing your answers.

1. After reading the four brief summaries of the four co-teaching approaches (supportive, parallel, complementary, team-teaching), answer the question posed in the text: "Under what circumstances can you envision using each of the four co-teaching approaches?" Be as specific as you can. For example, think about particular lessons that you have already taught or will be teaching and how the co-teaching approaches might be incorporated into them.

2. The authors use a marriage analogy to emphasize that co-teaching partnerships develop over time and with experience. In this chapter, they remind us of the old saying, "Although we get together on the basis of our similarities, we grow because of our differences." What are three or four ways that you and any of your co-teaching partners could grow because of your differences?

3. After reading about the three co-teaching teams that are featured in the book, what do you believe will be each team's greatest challenges when they begin co-teaching? What would be incentives or motivations for the partners of the three teams to co-teach?

Practical Applications

1. Review text Table 3.2, Co-Teaching Issues for Discussion and Planning. Think about someone with whom you currently co-teach or someone you wish to or will co-teach with in the future. With this person in mind, using the Issues to Discuss template presented in Handout 5, generate two or three questions per category that you want to pose and come to agreement on with your current or prospective co-teacher.

2. Repeat the above activity but this time with the person with whom you will or currently co-teach. If time is short, set a time in the future when you can brainstorm and come to agreement on answers to the questions.

3. Review text Table 3.3, Sample Co-Teaching Roles and Responsibilities Matrix. Based upon the roles and responsibilities that you and your co-teacher(s) must share, create your own personalized matrix that reflects the areas in which you will need to adjust responsibilities across the school year.

Activities for Workshop Facilitators and Course Instructors

There are two activities that facilitators can choose to offer participants: (1) Issues to Discuss and (2) Video/DVD Activity—The Day-to-Day Workings of Co-Teaching Teams.

● *Activity #1. Issues to Discuss*

Time: 10 minutes
Materials:

Handout 5: Advance Organizer: Issues for Discussion, one copy per participant

Directions:

1. Distribute Handout 5: Advance Organizer: Issues for Discussion. Tell participants that the categories on the handout are the areas in which all new co-teaching partners must pose and answer questions. Model what a question or issue might be in a couple of the categories. Feel free to use any issue from Table 3.2, Issues for Discussion and Planning, found in the book, as your example.

2. Group participants into triads. If co-teaching partners are together in the workshop, have them partner up with one another rather than someone who is not their co-teacher. Tell them they have six minutes to generate at least two questions or issues per category. Emphasize that the questions should be ones most critical for agreement before beginning co-teaching. Also, remind them that they are not yet answering these questions but merely posing them. They will have time to answer them later with their real co-teaching partners, when they will have more time to consider options.

3. Warn them at five minutes that they should have at least two questions per category. Stop them after six minutes and thank them for their work. Ask them to thank their partners.

4. Sample a response or two for each category, as time permits.

5. Ask if anyone thought of another category that was not on the "Issues for Discussion and Planning" table. If so, have them share it with the class. Acknowledge all new categories as valid.

6. Tell participants that you have one more category for them to add to their list as well—a new category titled "Pet Peeves" (Friend, 2008). Ask them to think about and write down what someone else does that they find annoying (e.g., underlines passages in books or teacher manuals, dog-ears teacher manuals, puts coffee cup on print materials and leaves coffee stains).

7. Ask if anyone has and would like to share a pet peeve. Tell them to be sure to bring up and get agreements about pet peeves with all current and future co-teaching partners.

● *Activity #2. The Day-to-Day Workings of Co-Teaching Teams*

Video/DVD Activity
Time: 30 minutes
Materials:

A computer or TV monitor and video/DVD player

Video/DVD cued to segment titled "The Day-to-Day Workings of Co-Teaching Teams"

Photocopies of Table 3.3, Co-Teaching Issues for Discussion and Planning, for each participant without the book

Directions:

1. Ask participants to turn to Table 3.3, Co-Teaching Issues for Discussion and Planning, in the book or in their handouts. Ask them to pretend they are coaches for the co-teaching teams shown in the video/DVD segment. In the role of coach, they will detect some of the issues, roles, and responsibilities that prospective co-teachers need to discuss. Ask participants to check off on Table 3.3 any of the questions that are discussed or answered by the teachers in the video.

2. Play the video/DVD segment titled "The Day-to-Day Workings of Co-Teaching Teams," in which elementary teachers talk about roles and responsibilities and fourth-grade co-teachers explain how they find the time to plan and solve problems.

3. After the video/DVD segment is complete, ask participants to turn to a neighbor and spend a minute or two exchanging observations.

4. Continue the video/DVD segment to allow participants to listen to middle school and high school teachers as they talk about the issues they must handle. Again, ask participants to check off on Table 3.3 any of the questions that are discussed or answered by the teachers in the video. When the video/DVD segment is complete, ask participants to turn to a different neighbor (i.e., to the other side or to the front or back) and spend another minute or two exchanging observations.

5. Ask three or four participants to share their observations.

6. Thank the participants for their observations and encourage them to use the questions in Table 3.3, Co-Teaching Issues for Discussion and Planning, as a resource for all first planning meetings with new co-teaching partners.

Part II: Four Approaches to Co-Teaching

Activity for Workshop Facilitators and Course Instructors

The four approaches can be previewed through the following activity, using the advance organizer for comparing and contrasting the four co-teaching approaches.

● *Activity #1. Compare and Contrast the Co-Teaching Approaches*

Time: 25 minutes
Materials:

Overhead transparency of Handout 6: Definitions of Co-Teaching Approaches

Photocopy for each participant of Handout 7: Similarities and Differences of Supportive, Parallel, Complementary, and Team-Teaching Co-Teaching Approaches

Directions:

1. Preview the four chapters included in Part II by putting up a transparency of Handout 6: Definitions of Co-Teaching Approaches. Have the participants read each of the definitions, pausing between each to ask for a show of hands if they think they have seen or used that approach.

2. Distribute Handout 7: Similarities and Differences of Supportive, Parallel, Complementary, and Team-Teaching Co-Teaching Approaches. Ask participants to keep this handout for use in examining Chapters 4 to 7. They will be completing sections of it as they learn more about the four approaches to co-teaching described in the chapters and shown in the corresponding video/DVD segment(s).

3. Ask participants to write down individually what they see as common characteristics across all four of the co-teaching approaches. Have them take a minute to share at least two commonalities with one or two neighbors. Ask the participants to share three or four commonalities. Thank them for their contributions and let them know they will look at commonalities again, as well as the unique features of and cautions in using each of the four approaches to co-teaching.

Chapter 4: The Supportive Co-Teaching Approach

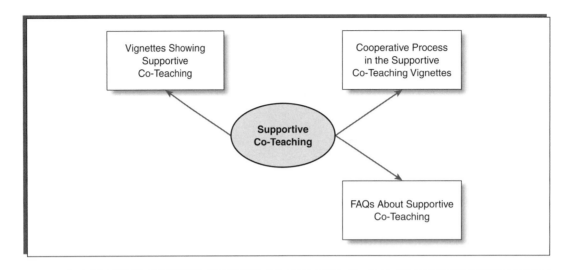

Figure 4.1   Content Map for Chapter 4

Summary

Supportive teaching is when one teacher takes the lead instructional role and the other(s) rotates among the students to provide support. In other words, one functions as a "sage on the stage" and the other as a "guide on the side." The co-teacher(s) taking the supportive role watches or listens as students work together and steps in to provide one-to-one tutorial assistance when necessary. The other co-teacher continues to direct the lesson. Both teachers have shared responsibility for all the students in the classroom.

Readers learn how to implement the supportive co-teaching approach effectively and how to avoid pitfalls through examples of the co-teaching teams introduced in Chapter 3 by actually using supportive co-teaching in lessons. This shows the rich array of organizational choices. The lessons are examined in terms of the five elements of the cooperative processes (i.e., face-to-face interaction, positive interdependence, interpersonal skills, monitoring, and accountability). The chapter ends with responses to frequently asked questions about the supportive co-teaching approach. A major caution when using the supportive co-teaching approach is that whoever is playing the support role (e.g., special educator, paraprofessional, or bilingual translator) must not become "Velcro-ed" to individual students, functioning as a hovercraft vehicle and blocking students' interactions with other students. Students and the support person(s) can be stigmatized if students perceive that the support teacher and those who are helped by the support teacher are not genuine members of the classroom. Supportive co-teachers must plan carefully so as to tap into the skills of the co-teacher who may have been locked into the supportive role. This allows both students and the support teacher to experience the benefits of co-teaching.

Discussion Questions

Decide what you would say in response to the following questions. You may work alone by writing your answers in a personal journal, or you may discuss your answers with a partner or teammates in a small group.

1. Have you used the supportive co-teaching approach or seen the supportive co-teaching approach being used? If so, share your experiences with your group members. If not, listen to those who have and ask one or two questions to clarify what supportive co-teaching is like.
2. Turn to the Frequently Asked Questions at the end of the chapter. Do *not* read the answers to the questions. Instead, read each question and compose your own answer. If you are working with a group, rotate the role of the reader for each of the questions. Compare your answers to each question, then read the response written in the text. In what ways were your responses similar or different? What new ideas did you get from the authors' response to each question?
3. Summarize the key points of this chapter through a role-play in which one teacher coaches another about how to use the supportive co-teaching approach. If you are working with a group, ask for volunteers to perform the role-plays. Celebrate your collective knowledge in individual quick-writes about what is most important to remember about the supportive co-teaching approach. Share your quick writes aloud with the entire group.

Practical Applications

1. Share your knowledge and skills by planning and co-teaching a supportive co-teaching lesson with a new partner.
2. Use modeling and guidance to assist another teacher, paraprofessional, or student teacher in your school or district in learning about and applying the supportive co-teaching approach.

Activities for Workshop Facilitators and Course Instructors

There are three activities that facilitators can offer participants: (1) Read and Apply, (2) Video/DVD Activity—The Supportive Co-Teaching Approach, and (3) Frequently Asked Questions and Cautions.

● *Activity #1. Read and Apply*

Time: 5–10 minutes
Materials:

Photocopy the first two paragraphs of Chapter 4 for each participant without a book. Ask participants who have the book to open to the first two paragraphs of Chapter 4.

Handout 7: Similarities and Differences of Supportive, Parallel, Complementary, and Team-Teaching Co-Teaching Approaches

Directions:

1. Ask participants to look at the matrix of Similarities and Differences of Supportive, Parallel, Complementary, and Team-Teaching Co-Teaching Approaches (Handout 7) they completed during the preview activity. Note: You have asked participants to keep this handout to use for Chapters 4 to 7. You may wish to have a few extra copies of the matrix should participants not bring their own copies from the preview activity.
2. Ask participants to read the first two paragraphs of the chapter, then individually write down what they consider to be the differences or unique characteristics of supportive co-teaching. Have them take a minute to share unique features with another participant. Ask for three or four characteristics from the group. Thank them for their contributions and let them know that they will look at cautions for this approach later in the workshop.

● *Activity #2. The Supportive Co-Teaching Approach*

Video/DVD Activity
Time: 20–30 minutes
Materials:

Video/DVD segment titled "The Supportive Co-Teaching Approach"

Handout 7: Similarities and Differences of Supportive, Parallel, Complementary, and Team-Teaching Co-Teaching Approaches

Directions:

1. Tell participants that in the first scene of this segment of the video/DVD, Steve and Stephanie (the general educator and special educator) are teaching a middle-level math class. The second scene shows Diane and Kathy co-teaching a language arts class. The third scene shows Trindo and her paraprofessional

in a different language arts class. The fourth scene shows Kathleen and Aimee co-teaching a biology class.

2. Direct participants to carefully observe the segment to detect how the supportive co-teaching approach is used. Ask participants to jot down their ideas about who takes the lead and who takes the supportive role. List the kinds of support each one is providing. The idea is to have some notes for your discussion of how the supportive co-teaching approach looks and sounds in a variety of settings.

3. After viewing the video/DVD segment, ask participants to divide into small groups and discuss what they observed. They should share examples of what supportive co-teaching looked and sounded like for each of the four scenes.

Notes to the facilitator: Steve explains the task, while Stephanie prompts individual participation. With Diane and Kathy, you see one teacher talking and writing on the board, while the other sits with students at selected tables. Then you see the co-teachers exchange roles, with the special educator taking the lead to teach the whole class and the general educator circulating to monitor students. In the segment with Trindo and her paraprofessional, Trindo takes the lead role, and the paraprofessional monitors individual students. In the biology class, you see Aimee taking the lead teacher role, while Kathleen quietly writes notes on the whiteboard; the notes will be used in the next section of the lesson.

● *Activity #3. Frequently Asked Questions and Cautions*

Time: 10–15 minutes
Materials:

Photocopy the "Frequently Asked Questions" section of Chapter 4 for each participant without a book. Ask participants who have the book to open to "Frequently Asked Questions" in Chapter 4.

Handout 7: Similarities and Differences of Supportive, Parallel, Complementary, and Team-Teaching Co-Teaching Approaches

Directions:

1. Turn to the "Frequently Asked Questions" at the end of the chapter. Do not read the answers to the questions. Instead, read each question and compose your own answer. If you are working with a group, rotate the role of the reader for each of the questions. Compare your answers to each question, then read the response written in the text. In what ways were your responses similar or different? What new ideas occurred to you when you read the authors' responses to the questions?

2. Have participants locate Handout 7: Similarities and Differences of Supportive, Parallel, Complementary, and Team-Teaching Co-Teaching Approaches matrix. Tell them that the "Frequently Asked Questions" and the answers to each of these questions, as well as the rest of Chapter 4, may help them think of some common pitfalls to avoid with supportive co-teaching. Ask them to record two or three cautions to use with supportive co-teaching in the "Supportive Cautions" section on the matrix.

3. Debrief by polling participants, asking them to share a few cautions. Listen for the following cautions named by the authors:
   - Beware of the "Velcro" or "hovercraft" effect of being attached to one student, as this can both stigmatize the student as being not a real member of the class and foster codependence.
   - Beware of one teacher becoming the discipline police, copier of class materials, or in-class paper grader.
   - Beware of becoming comfortable in the supportive role based on lack of time to plan.
   - Beware of not using the skills of another educator locked into the supportive role.
   - Beware of potential resentment from a co-teacher locked into the supportive role or from the lead teacher feeling she carries the burden of the workload.

4. If participants do not identify all five of these cautions, describe the remaining cautions so that they can be added to the "Similarities and Differences of Co-Teaching" graphic organizer.

Chapter 5: The Parallel Co-Teaching Approach

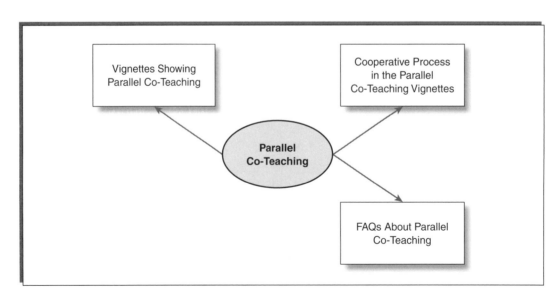

Figure 5.1   Content Map for Chapter 5

Summary

Parallel teaching occurs when two or more people work with different groups of students in different sections of the classroom. Parallel co-teaching has many faces, including the following: (1) split class, (2) station teaching or learning centers, (3) co-teachers rotating to groups of students, (4) cooperative group monitoring, (5) supervising experiments or lab activities, (6) learning styles (e.g., auditory, visual, kinesthetic), and (7) supplementary instruction.

Readers learn how to implement the parallel co-teaching approach effectively through the examples of the elementary, middle, and high school co-teaching teams, introduced in Chapter 3, actually using parallel co-teaching approaches in lessons. The lessons are examined in terms of the five elements of the cooperative processes (face-to-face interaction, positive interdependence, interpersonal skills, monitoring, and accountability). The chapter ends with responses to three frequently asked questions about the parallel co-teaching approach.

Be aware of two cautions when implementing the parallel co-teaching approach. First, guard against creating a special class within your class. This can happen when co-teachers routinely group the same students into the same group with the same co-teacher. Second, guard against the homogeneous grouping of students. When low-performing students are grouped with other low-performing students, their assessed performance can drop dramatically (Marzano, Pickering, & Pollack, 2001). Rotating students among instructors avoids the stigmatization that may arise if someone other than the classroom teacher (e.g., special educator, paraprofessional) only teaches one set of students.

Discussion Questions

Decide what you would say to the following questions. You may work alone by responding in a personal journal, or you may discuss your answers with a partner or teammates in a group-discussion format.

1. Imagine that you are having a conversation with a school board member who has heard about the parallel co-teaching approach and has asked you to explain it. What are the two most important things about parallel co-teaching approaches that you would tell this board member?
2. Have you used any parallel co-teaching approaches, or have you seen others use any parallel co-teaching approaches? If so, share your experiences with your group members.
3. Turn to the "Frequently Asked Questions" section at the end of the chapter. Do not read the answers to the questions. Instead, read each question and compose your own answer. If you are

working with a group, rotate the role of reader for each of the questions. Compare your answers to each question, then read the response written in the text. In what ways were your responses similar or different? What new ideas did you get from the authors' response to each question?

Practical Applications

1. Work with your school or district professional development staff to start a study group for the purpose of generating recommendations on implementing the parallel co-teaching approach, if it is not being practiced in your district already.
2. Observe other educators using parallel co-teaching and subsequently, when they debrief, listen to their reflections about their co-taught lesson.
3. Try one of the parallel co-teaching approaches listed in Table 5.1 from the book with another educator. Notice what happens to student engagement and performance or achievement. What happened to your sense of achievement and your attitudes about this parallel co-teaching approach?
4. Systematically try out each of the other parallel co-teaching approaches listed in Table 5.1.
5. Share your knowledge and skills by planning and co-teaching with a new partner. Use modeling and guidance to assist another teacher, paraprofessional, or student teacher in your school or district in implementing some of the parallel co-teaching approaches.

Activities for Workshop Facilitators and Course Instructors

There are four activities that facilitators can offer participants to master the content of Chapter 5: (1) Read and Apply, (2) The Many Faces of Parallel Co-Teaching, (3) Video/DVD Activity—The Parallel Co-Teaching Approach, and (4) Frequently Asked Questions and Cautions.

● *Activity #1. Read and Apply*

Time: 5–10 minutes
Materials:

Photocopy the first two paragraphs of Chapter 5 for each participant without a book. Ask participants who have the book to open to the first two paragraphs of Chapter 5.

Handout 7: Similarities and Differences of Supportive, Parallel, Complementary, and Team-Teaching Co-Teaching Approaches

Directions:

1. Ask participants to look at the Similarities and Differences of Supportive, Parallel, Complementary, and Team-Teaching Co-Teaching Approaches matrix (Handout 7), which they completed in the preview activity. Note: You have asked participants to keep this handout for use in examining Chapters 4 to 7. You may wish to have a few extra copies of the matrix should participants not bring their own copies from the preview activity.

2. Ask participants to read the first two paragraphs of the chapter, then individually write down what they consider to be the differences or unique characteristics of parallel co-teaching. Have them take a minute to share unique features with another participant. Ask three or four participants to share characteristics. Thank them for their contributions and let them know that they will look at cautions later in the workshop.

● *Activity #2. The Many Faces of Parallel Co-Teaching*

Time: 10 minutes
Materials:

Photocopy Table 5.1, Examples of Parallel Teaching Structures with Co-Teachers Teaching the Same or Different Content, for each participant without a book. Ask participants who have the book to open to Table 5.1.

Directions:

1. Organize participants in pairs or triads and have them read, one at a time, each of the seven structures of parallel co-teaching presented in Table 5.1.

2. Instruct participants to read the first structure (i.e., split class) silently, then discuss how they have used or could use this structure in future lessons. Ask them to be as specific as possible so their partners can picture exactly how the structure would be used in the lesson. Allow them one minute to read and discuss examples of the first structure.

3. Tell participants to repeat the above process for all seven structures. They will have seven minutes to read and share examples of how to use all seven structures.

4. Debrief by naming each structure and saying, "As I name each structure, please raise your hand if this parallel approach

is either new to you or one that you found attractive and might like to try in future lessons." If time permits, ask people to share the benefits to using their favorite parallel co-teaching structure(s).

● *Activity #3. The Parallel Co-Teaching Approach*

Video/DVD Activity
Time: 20–30 minutes
Materials:

Video/DVD segment titled "The Parallel Co-Teaching Approach," which shows scenes of parallel co-teaching approaches in elementary, middle, and high school classrooms

Photocopy Table 5.1, Examples of Parallel Teaching Structures With Co-Teachers Teaching the Same or Different Content, for each participant without a book. Ask participants who have the book to open to Table 5.1.

Directions:

1. Tell participants they will see a few of the ways to structure parallel co-teaching described in the book. Ask them to look at Table 5.1, which describes seven "faces," or structures, of parallel co-teaching (this was used in the first activity). Tell them they will be watching four parallel co-teaching lessons on the video/DVD. Ask them to note which of the seven structures each of the four teams used and also exactly what each person was doing in a parallel co-teaching role.

2. Play the four scenes of the video/DVD segment. You may choose to pause between each example to have the participants jot down notes as to the structure(s) used or to talk with other participants. You also may choose to play all seven minutes of the segment and then have the participants look at Table 5.1 to identify and describe the parallel co-teaching structures they observed.

3. Ask participants to share their observations of the different roles of the co-teachers for each parallel co-teaching structure in the video/DVD.

4. Ask participants to think of one or two examples of when they might use a parallel co-teaching structure to teach their students. If there is time, have participants share with a neighbor and then ask volunteers to share what their neighbor described.

● *Activity #4. Frequently Asked Questions and Cautions*

Time: 10–15 minutes
Materials:

Photocopy the "Frequently Asked Questions" section of Chapter 5 for each participant without a book. Ask participants who have the book to open to the "Frequently Asked Questions" section of Chapter 5.

Handout 7: Similarities and Differences of Supportive, Parallel, Complementary, and Team-Teaching Co-Teaching Approaches

Directions:

1. Turn to "Frequently Asked Questions" at the end of the chapter. Do not read the answers to the questions. Instead read each question and compose your own answer. If you are working with a group, rotate the role of reader for each of the questions. Compare your answers to each question, then read the response written in the text. In what ways were your responses similar or different? What new ideas did you get from the authors' response to each question?

2. Have participants locate Handout 7: Similarities and Differences of Supportive, Parallel, Complementary, and Team-Teaching Co-Teaching Approaches matrix. Tell them that "Frequently Asked Questions" and the answers to each of these questions, as well as the rest of Chapter 5, may help them think of some common pitfalls to avoid with parallel co-teaching. Ask them to record two or three cautions to use with parallel co-teaching in the Parallel Cautions section on the matrix.

3. Debrief by sampling a few cautions from participants. Listen for the following cautions:
   • Beware of creating a special class-within-the-class, thereby lowering student achievement, by homogeneously grouping lower-performing students together (Marzano et al., 2001, p. 84).
   • Beware that the noise level can become uncomfortably high when numerous activities are occurring in the same room.
   • Beware of failing to prepare other co-teachers adequately to ensure they deliver instruction as intended, because you cannot monitor each other while you are simultaneously co-teaching.

4. If participants do not identify all three of the above cautions, share with them the remaining cautions so they can be added to the Similarities and Differences of Co-Teaching graphic organizer.

Chapter 6: The Complementary Co-Teaching Approach

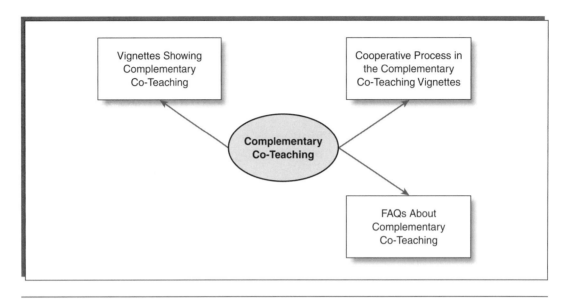

Figure 6.1   Content Map for Chapter 6

Summary

Complementary co-teaching involves two or more adults who are interacting with all of the children in the same class. Both teachers are "on stage," and one teacher does something to enhance the instruction provided by the other teacher. For example, co-teachers may vary how a lesson is delivered (e.g., one describes, and the other writes; one reads aloud, while the other shows students how to follow along using a lecture guide). Readers learn how to implement the complementary co-teaching approach effectively through examples of the elementary, middle, and high school co-teaching teams introduced in Chapter 3. The lessons are analyzed in terms of the five elements of the cooperative processes (face-to-face interaction, positive interdependence, interpersonal skills, monitoring, and accountability). The chapter ends with responses to two frequently asked questions about the complementary co-teaching approach.

Discussion Questions

Decide what you would say in response to the following questions. You may work alone by responding in a personal journal, or you may discuss your answers with a partner or teammates in a small group.

1. In what ways have you implemented (or might you implement) the complementary co-teaching approach in one of the classes you teach?

2. Turn to "Frequently Asked Questions" at the end of the chapter. Do not read the answers to each question. Instead, read each question and compose your own answer. If you are working with a group, rotate the role of reader for each question. Compare your answers to each question, then read the response written in the text. In what ways were your responses similar or different? What new ideas did you get from the authors' response to each question?

Practical Applications

1. Observe a co-teaching lesson where the complementary co-teaching approach is being used. Sit with the co-teachers as they plan and/or reflect upon the lesson. What did you learn about how the co-teachers complement one another's instruction?
2. Try planning and carrying out a complementary co-teaching lesson with another educator. Notice what happens with student engagement and performance or achievement. What feelings did you have about sharing the teacher role as you planned and delivered instruction as team teachers?
3. Share your knowledge and skills about complementary co-teaching with another teacher, paraprofessional, or student teacher in your school or district. Use modeling and coaching to help that colleague initiate, deliver, and reflect upon complementary co-teaching.

Activities for Workshop Facilitators and Course Instructors

There are three activities that facilitators can offer participants to master the content of Chapter 6: (1) Read and Apply, (2) Video/DVD Activity—The Complementary Co-Teaching Approach, and (3) Frequently Asked Questions and Cautions.

● *Activity #1. Read and Apply*

Time: 5–10 minutes
Materials:

Photocopy the first three paragraphs of Chapter 6 for each participant without a book. Ask participants who have a copy of the book to open to the first three paragraphs of Chapter 6.

Handout 7: Similarities and Differences of Supportive, Parallel, Complementary, and Team-Teaching Co-Teaching Approaches

Directions:

1. Ask participants to look at the matrix titled "Similarities and Differences of Supportive, Parallel, Complementary, and Team-Teaching Co-Teaching Approaches" (Handout 7) that they completed during the preview activity. Note: You have asked participants to keep the matrix to use for Chapters 4 to 7. You may wish to have a few extra copies of the matrix should participants not bring their own copies from the preview activity.

2. Ask participants to read the first three paragraphs of the chapter, then individually write down what they consider to be the differences or unique characteristics of complementary co-teaching. Have them take a minute to share unique features with another participant. Ask three or four participants to share characteristics with the entire group. Thank them for their contributions and let them know that they will look at cautions later in the workshop.

● *Activity #2. The Complementary Co-Teaching Approach*

Video/DVD Activity
Time: 20–30 minutes
Materials:

Video/DVD segment titled "The Complementary Co-Teaching Approach"

Video player with TV monitor and/or DVD player

Directions:

1. Tell participants they will watch co-teachers in elementary, middle, and high school classrooms so they can see what complementary co-teaching looks and sounds like.
2. Tell them to be prepared to answer the following questions after watching the video/DVD:
   • Why are these examples of complementary co-teaching rather than parallel or supportive co-teaching?
   • What did you see or hear that makes the distinctions?
   • What effective instructional practices did you see?
   • How did the co-teachers coordinate their actions and support one another?
3. Play the video/DVD segment titled "The Complementary Co-Teaching Approach."
4. When the video segment is complete, ask participants to discuss with a neighbor the answers to the questions posed in Step 2. Provide them with eight minutes to discuss all four questions, prompting them to move on to the second question after two minutes and the third after approximately four minutes.

5. Debrief participants' observations by sampling responses to the questions.

● *Activity #3. Frequently Asked Questions and Cautions*

Time: 10–15 minutes
Materials:

Photocopy the "Frequently Asked Questions" section of Chapter 6 for each participant without a book. Ask participants who have the book to open to "Frequently Asked Questions" in Chapter 6.

Handout 7: Similarities and Differences of Supportive, Parallel, Complementary, and Team-Teaching Co-Teaching Approaches

Directions:

1. Turn to "Frequently Asked Questions" at the end of the chapter. Do not read the answers to the questions. Instead, read each question and compose your own answer. If you are working with a group, rotate the role of reader for each of the questions. Compare your answers to each question, then read the response written in the text. In what ways were your responses similar or different? What new ideas did you get from the authors' response to each question?

2. Have participants locate Handout 7: Similarities and Differences of Supportive, Parallel, Complementary, and Team-Teaching Co-Teaching Approaches matrix. Tell them that "Frequently Asked Questions" and the answers to each of these questions, as well as the rest of Chapter 6, will help them think of some common pitfalls to avoid with complementary co-teaching. Ask them to record two or three cautions to be used with complementary co-teaching in the "Complementary Cautions" section on the matrix.

3. Debrief by polling participants to share a few of the cautions. Listen for the following cautions:
   • Beware of not monitoring the students who need it.
   • Beware of too much teacher talk, repetition, and lack of student-to-student interaction.
   • Beware of typecasting the co-teacher delivering content as the "expert" or "real" teacher.
   • Beware of failing to plan for "role release," so all co-teachers get to teach the content.

4. If participants do not identify all four of the above cautions, share with them the remaining cautions so they can be added to the "Similarities and Differences of Co-Teaching" graphic organizer.

Chapter 7: The Team-Teaching Co-Teaching Approach

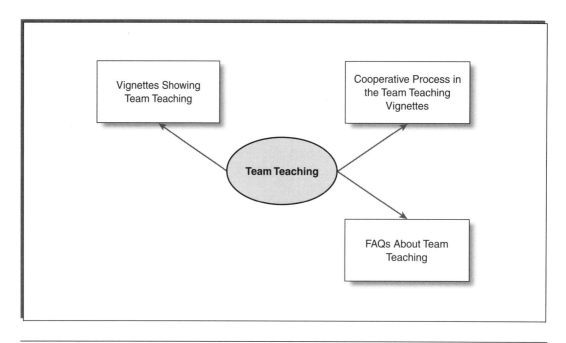

Figure 7.1 Content Map for Chapter 7

Summary

Team teaching is defined by the authors as "two or more people with differing expertise who do what the traditional teacher used to do." Team teachers share the responsibility for planning, teaching, and assessing progress of the same students in the class(es) that they team-teach. In this chapter, you will see the co-teaching team of Ms. Gilpatrick and Ms. Nugent (an elementary school teacher and a speech/language therapist, respectively) using the SODAS problem-solving process in a class meeting; the middle-level team (i.e., science teacher, special educator, and paraprofessional) adapting the Multiple Intelligences Theory to individualize instruction for a science project; and Mr. Woo (a social studies teacher) and Mr. Viana (a special educator) planning, for their high school students, a two-week lesson about the primaries, campaign finances, conventions, and election processes used in the United States. The elements of the cooperative process are highlighted for each team. Finally, frequently asked questions about team teaching are posed and answered. One response proposes a co-teaching taxonomy where Vygotzgy's Zone of Proximal Development (ZPD) is used to explain how teachers gradually shift from an attitude of avoidance to an attitude of appreciation for all four co-teaching approaches.

Discussion Questions

Decide what you would say in response to the following questions. You may work alone by responding in a personal journal, or you may discuss your answers with a partner or teammates in a small group.

1. Identify three ideas you gleaned from reading the three co-teaching examples in this chapter that you can use in structuring team-taught lessons.
2. In what ways have you implemented—or might you implement in the future—team teaching with another teacher, specialist, or paraprofessional?
3. Turn to "Frequently Asked Questions" at the end of the chapter. Do not read the answers to the questions. Instead, read the questions and compose your own answers. If you are working with a group, rotate the role of reader for each of the questions. Compare your answers to each question, then read the response written in the text. In what ways were your responses similar or different? What new ideas did you get from the authors' response to each question?
4. It takes time for co-teaching partners to get to know one another and be most effective at using the team-teaching co-teaching approach. What are some factors you believe contribute to a better team-teaching partnership? Identify three or four factors and, if you are in a group, share and compare them with your group members. Then read about the taxonomy for co-teaching described in the chapter as the authors' response to the second question in "Frequently Asked Questions." In what ways might this taxonomy relate to the factors that you identified as promoting effective team teaching? How does this taxonomy help you work better with other teachers to implement the four co-teaching approaches, including team teaching?

Practical Applications

1. Observe co-teachers who use the team-teaching co-teaching approach. Sit in on their planning and/or reflection meeting(s). In what ways have they distributed the role of one teacher across all the members of their team?
2. Teach the SODAS problem-solving process to your students using the lesson plan described in the elementary school example in Chapter 7 and the SODAS Template shown as Handout 8. Teach the sample team-teaching lesson in the Resource B appendix.
3. Ask someone to plan and team-teach a lesson with you in the upcoming weeks. Deliver the lesson and notice your feelings,

thoughts, and opinions as you plan and teach the lesson. Share what you noticed with your team-teaching partner. How can you use this information to further advance your co-teaching relationship and improve instruction?

4. Exchange with other teachers a videotape of your team-taught lesson so you and your team-teaching colleague(s) can give and receive coaching on how to improve your team-teaching skills.

Activities for Workshop Facilitators and Course Instructors

There are three activities that facilitators can offer participants to master the content of Chapter 7: (1) Read and Apply, (2) Video/DVD Activity—The Team-Teaching Co-Teaching Approach, and (3) Frequently Asked Questions and Cautions.

● *Activity #1. Read and Apply*

Time: 5–10 minutes
Materials:

Photocopy the first three paragraphs of Chapter 7 for each participant without a book. Ask participants who have a copy of the book to open to the first three paragraphs of Chapter 7.

Handout 7: Similarities and Differences of Supportive, Parallel, Complementary, and Team-Teaching Co-Teaching Approaches

Directions:

1. Ask participants to look at the "Similarities and Differences of Supportive, Parallel, Complementary, and Team-Teaching Co-Teaching Approaches" (Handout 7) matrix completed during the preview activity. Note: You have asked participants to keep this handout to use with Chapters 4 to 7. You may wish to have a few extra copies of the matrix should participants not bring their own copies from the previous activity.

2. Ask participants to read the first three paragraphs of the chapter, then individually write down what they consider to be the differences or unique characteristics of team teaching as compared to the other three co-teaching approaches (supportive, parallel, and complementary).

3. Debrief by having participants share unique features with another participant or two. Ask for three or four volunteers to share examples of characteristics.

● *Activity #2. The Team-Teaching Co-Teaching Approach*

Video/DVD Activity
Time: 20–30 minutes
Materials:

Video/DVD cued to segment titled "The Team-Teaching Co-Teaching Approach"

Video player with TV monitor and/or DVD player

Directions:

1. Tell participants that this video/DVD segment shows how elementary- and middle-level co-teaching teams use team teaching. Prior to showing the video/DVD, tell participants to look for ways in which the teaching teams shared responsibility for planning, teaching, and assessing the students they share.
2. Play the video/DVD segment titled "The Team-Teaching Co-Teaching Approach." At the end of the four-minute elementary-level segment, stop the video/DVD. Ask participants to think about the question, "How did these teachers share responsibility for planning, teaching, and assessing their shared students?" Give them a minute to write down examples from the video/DVD and then have them discuss their observations with a partner.
3. After two or three minutes of discussion, reconvene the entire group to continue watching the video/DVD example for middle-level team teachers.
4. When this segment is complete, ask participants to discuss their observations with a different partner. Ask them to focus on how the two teachers shared responsibilities and roles as team teachers.
5. After one or two minutes, debrief as a whole group by asking participants to voice examples of how the co-teachers shared responsibilities.

● *Activity #3. Frequently Asked Questions and Cautions*

Time: 25–30 minutes
Materials:

Photocopy "Frequently Asked Questions" from Chapter 7 for each participant without a book. Ask participants who have the book to open to "Frequently Asked Questions" in Chapter 7.

Handout 7: Similarities and Differences of Supportive, Parallel, Complementary, and Team-Teaching Co-Teaching Approaches

Directions:

1. Tell the participants to turn to "Frequently Asked Questions" at the end of Chapter 7 and read the first question. Instruct them to not read the answer to the question but instead come up with their own answers. Arrange participants into pairs or triads and have one person be the reader and another person be the recorder. Tell them that once they have two or three possible answers, they may read the answer in the text. After they have read the authors' answer, have them respond to these questions: (1) In what ways were your responses similar or different? and (2) What new ideas did you learn from the authors' response to this question?

2. To introduce the second question in "Frequently Asked Questions," tell participants, "It takes time for co-teaching partners to get to know one another and to be effective at using the team-teaching co-teaching approach. What are some factors you believe contribute to becoming a better team-teaching partnership? Identify three or four factors and, if you are in a group, share and compare them with your group members." Give them some time to identify three or four factors. Then ask them to read the answer to the second question, in which the authors describe the co-teaching taxonomy. After all participants have read the answer, ask pairs or triads to discuss the following two questions: (1) In what ways does this taxonomy relate to the factors that you identified as promoting effective team teaching? and (2) How does this taxonomy help you to work better with other teachers to implement the four co-teaching approaches, including team teaching? After two or three minutes of small-group discussion of these questions, debrief by having participants share the answers.

3. Have participants locate the "Similarities and Differences of Supportive, Parallel, Complementary, and Team-Teaching Co-Teaching Approaches" (Handout 7) matrix. Tell them that "Frequently Asked Questions" and the answers to each of these questions, as well as the rest of Chapter 7, may help them think of some common pitfalls to avoid with team-teaching co-teaching. In the same groups as for the previous activity, have them discuss and record two or three cautions to be used when team teaching in the "Team-Teaching Cautions" section on the matrix.

4. Sample the participants' cautions. Note that the cautions are similar to those for complementary co-teaching. A particular caution for team teachers is to guard against getting too comfortable with the same roles or division of labor. One of the benefits of team teaching is that co-teachers can exchange and rearrange roles to get practice with new instructional strategies

and to increase understanding and mastery in teaching all aspects of the content (e.g., the special educator becomes proficient at teaching algebraic concepts and procedures by taking the lead on the instruction of the content; the mathematics teacher becomes more proficient at taking on the special educator's traditional role of differentiating materials and assignments, preparing visual aids, and using vocabulary development methodologies). This can only occur if co-teachers periodically "switch it up" and trade off, or rearrange, the division of labor.

Integration Activities

All Four Approaches to Co-Teaching

Use the following three activities to integrate the information presented in Chapters 4 to 7 on the four approaches to co-teaching: (1) Compare and Contrast the Four Approaches to Co-Teaching, (2) Dance Co-Teaching, and (3) Steve and Stephanie—Compare and Contrast Team Teaching With Other Co-Teaching Approaches.

● *Activity #1. Compare and Contrast the Four Approaches to Co-Teaching*

Time: 20 minutes
Materials:

Handout 6: Definitions of Co-Teaching Approaches

Participants' notes regarding similarities, differences, and cautions for each of the four approaches to co-teaching recorded on the Handout 7: "Similarities and Differences of Supportive, Parallel, Complementary, and Team-Teaching Co-Teaching Approaches" matrix

A blank overhead and one additional copy for each participant of Handout 7: Similarities and Differences of Supportive, Parallel, Complementary, and Team-Teaching Co-Teaching Approaches

Overhead projector and overhead markers

The facilitator prepares for this activity by (1) reviewing the first two or three paragraphs of each of Chapters 4 to 7, which describe the unique features of each of the approaches, and (2) reviewing the list of cautions at the end of the last workshop activity for Chapters 4 to 7.

Directions:

1. Ask participants to find the notes they have taken on the similarities and differences of the four co-teaching approaches and the cautions for each approach as you pass out to each participant a new, blank template of the Handout 7 matrix.

2. Tell participants they now have the opportunity to summarize what they have learned about all four approaches to co-teaching. Direct them to think about the readings, activities, and video/DVD viewings in which they have engaged for the supportive, parallel, complementary, and team-teaching co-teaching approaches and then complete the similarities section of the matrix.

3. After one or two minutes, ask participants to exchange papers with a neighbor and "interview" the neighbor about the similarities they each noticed among all four approaches.

4. After one or two minutes, reconvene the entire group and solicit similarities from the participants, asking them to share either their own or their partner's ideas. If they have trouble coming up with similarities, you may prompt them with suggestions such as the following:
   a. Two or more instructors (e.g., teachers, paraprofessionals, student teachers, community volunteers) in the classroom
   b. Capitalizes upon specific strengths and expertise of co-teachers
   c. Increases the teacher/student ratio and introduces additional support for students in the classroom
   d. Requires time for planning, more so as co-teachers move from supportive co-teaching through the other approaches to team teaching
   e. Shares, in varying degrees, the responsibility for planning, teaching, and assessing some or all of the students in the class; the responsibility becomes increasingly co-equal as co-teachers move from supportive to team-teaching approaches
   f. Benefits students with different backgrounds through bringing diverse teaching styles to the classroom and the "two heads are better than one" aspect of having more than one instructor

5. Ask participants to find two or three other workshop participants with whom they have not yet had a chance to work in the Chapters 4 to 7 activities. Tell them they have eight minutes to fill in the remaining eight cells on the matrix; that is, to describe the unique features or differences of each of the four co-teaching approaches and to identify cautions for each of the four approaches. Monitor by walking around and listening to the groups as they work. At the four-minute mark, give them a "four-minute warning," urging them to move on to the remaining cells of the matrix so they have notes in all eight cells.

6. Debrief the differences among the co-teaching approaches first by sampling and recording on the overhead one or two of the key features of each of the approaches and one or two of the major cautions. As you debrief the unique features and differences of the four approaches, show Handout 6: Definitions of Co-Teaching Approaches, on the overhead projector to help them think about ideas related to unique features. For parallel co-teaching, remind them that there are at least seven faces of parallel co-teaching, which they examined in Chapter 5.

7. Prepare for the debriefing of the cautions by reviewing the last activity in Chapters 4 to 7, which lists the cautions for each of the co-teaching approaches. Compile these cautions into a list so you have them to record on the overhead should the participants have trouble coming up with a list of cautions.

● *Activity #2. Dance Co-Teaching*

Time: 10–15 minutes
Directions:

1. The authors suggest that dance can be a metaphor for the subtle differences among the four approaches to co-teaching. Many co-teachers feel as though they are dancing around each other (watching out that they don't step on each other's toes, for example, or notice when their partner wants to add something spontaneously to the lesson). Work with a partner and discuss between the two of you the type of dance that best represents each of the four approaches to co-teaching. You might ask each other the following questions:
   a. In what kind of dance does one partner lead and the other follow?
   b. In what kind of dance do partners do their own thing?
   c. In what kind of dance does one partner's move complement the moves of the other partner?
   d. In what kind of dance do the partners show sophistication, complexity, creativity, and intimacy?

2. Ask participants to dance their selections and explain why they selected each dance type to represent each of the four co-teaching approaches. For example, for team teaching, Jacque and Rich dance the tango, explaining, "The team-teaching approach is like dancing a tango because of the intimacy, sophistication, complexity, creativity, and anticipation of each other's moves. Plus, if you get a new partner, you are less likely to be able to anticipate that person's moves, as they are unfamiliar to you. You may end up stepping on that person's toes as a result."

● *Activity #3. Steven and Stephanie—Compare and Contrast Team Teaching With Other Co-Teaching Approaches*

Video/DVD Activity
Time: 15 minutes
Materials:

Handout 1: Definition of Co-Teaching

The four video/DVD segments of the middle-level math team, Steve and Stephanie, showing them using the supportive, parallel, complementary, and team-teaching co-teaching approaches

Video player with TV monitor and/or DVD player

Directions:

1. Display the overhead of brief definitions of the four co-teaching approaches (Handout 1) and quickly review the definitions. Now that the participants have studied and viewed video/DVD segments showing all four co-teaching approaches in action, it would be interesting to contrast their use of supportive, parallel, and complementary co-teaching with team teaching. They will be watching the middle-level math team of Steve and Stephanie as they use all four co-teaching approaches, beginning with supportive and progressing to team teaching. Before showing the segments, ask participants to note, as they watch the video, how this co-teaching team deliberately chose to use each of the four co-teaching approaches at particular points in their instruction. Tell the participants, "As you watch the two teachers in action, think about why they chose this particular co-teaching approach to support students. In what ways does or could this co-teaching approach benefit the students and facilitate access to the mathematics curriculum? In what ways does this co-teaching approach benefit the co-teachers?"

2. View the supportive co-teaching video/DVD segment of Steve and Stephanie. When the segment is complete, have participants form groups of no more than four people, working with someone with whom they have not interacted (if possible). Give them three to four minutes to discuss two questions: (1) In what ways does or could this co-teaching approach benefit the students and facilitate access to the mathematics curriculum? (2) In what ways does this co-teaching approach benefit the co-teachers?

3. Repeat the above process for the parallel, complementary, and team teaching co-teaching video/DVD segments.

4. Bring closure to this final activity in Part II by telling participants they now are experts in the four co-teaching approaches and they are ready to use all four approaches effectively, as well as teach someone else about them. Ask group members first to thank one another for their thoughtful conversation. Next, ask them to engage in the processing technique of "Strength Bombardment," in which each team member receives compliments from the others about their contributions to the discussion of Steve and Stephanie implementing all four co-teaching approaches.

Part III: Changing Roles and Responsibilities

Chapter 8: The Role of Paraprofessionals in Co-Teaching

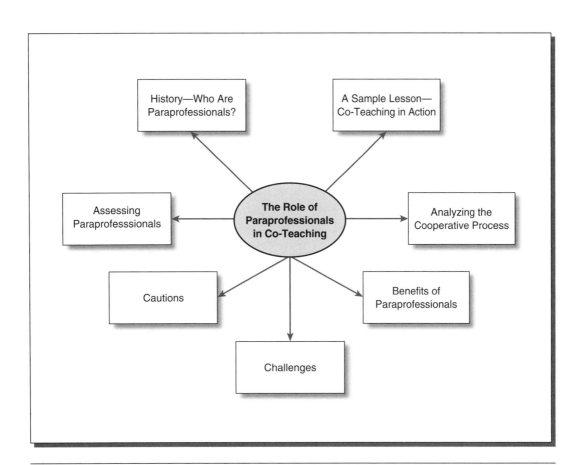

Figure 8.1   Content Map for Chapter 8

Summary

In Chapter 8, the authors first examine the roles of paraprofessionals by sharing a brief history of paraprofessionals in U.S. schools. In the 1950s, they played primarily clerical roles; today, they are critical members of the instructional team. Paraprofessionals' various job titles—teaching assistant, instructional aide, educational technician—reflect the changes in and the diversity of the roles paraprofessionals play in the education of children.

Next, you meet a co-teaching team as they prepare to co-teach, plan a series of lessons, and then implement the lessons. You also are reminded of the roles of other paraprofessionals from co-teaching teams described in Chapter 2 (i.e., Ms. Hernandez is a member of the elementary school co-teaching team; Ms. Olvina works with Mr. Silva, a middle school teacher, for his math and science classes). You discover from the examples that it is possible for paraprofessionals to provide meaningful instruction in all four co-teaching arrangements.

A feature of this chapter is the discussion of the benefits paraprofessionals bring to today's diverse classrooms. Namely, paraprofessionals support the inclusion of students with disabilities and the differentiation of instruction for *all* students. They can serve as ambassadors for families from culturally and linguistically diverse heritages. They also are a source for recruiting teachers who represent the cultural and linguistic characteristics of the schools in which they work.

Challenges faced by paraprofessionals and their supervisors include poorly defined role definitions, ambiguity in supervisory responsibilities, and inconsistent initial and ongoing professional development. The chapter ends with cautions for paraprofessionals working in each of the four co-teaching approaches and a call for professional development and coaching based upon some standard, such as a clear paraprofessional job description.

Discussion Questions

Decide what you would say in response to the following questions. You may work alone by responding in a personal journal, or you may discuss your answers with a partner or teammates in a small group.

1. After reading about the co-teaching team featured in this chapter, which includes the versatile paraprofessional, Ms. Katz, reflect on the following question: Under what conditions do you believe

paraprofessionals can be effective in each of the co-teaching roles—supportive, parallel, complementary, and team teaching?

2. In your opinion, why, in the section of the chapter that examines poor role definition for paraprofessionals, do the authors say that "role flexibility is both a gift and a burden?"

Practical Applications

1. Use the Self-Assessment: *Are We Really Co-Teachers?* checklist presented in Table 11.4 in the book with a paraprofessional with whom you are working. Talk about the results and set one or two short-term goals.

2. Imagine that you are having a conversation with a group of parents who are concerned about the qualifications of the para-professional who works in your classroom. What would you say to them to explain the benefits your paraprofessional brings to you, the children, and the school?

3. Imagine that you are a member of a co-teaching team where you have become accustomed to using all four approaches to co-teaching. Your administrator tells you that a paraprofessional fluent in sign language will join your team to support a new student class member who is deaf. Describe three important ground rules of which you want the paraprofessional and her supervisor to be aware before she starts to work with your team.

4. Observe a co-taught lesson where a paraprofessional is co-teaching with a general or special educator. Sit in on and listen to the co-teachers' conversation as the teacher and para-professional reflect upon the lesson.

Activities for Workshop Facilitators and Course Instructors

There are four activities that facilitators can offer participants to master the content of Chapter 8: (1) Benefits and Challenges Jigsaw, (2) Vignette Analysis, (3) Video/DVD Activity—The Role of the Paraprofessional in Co-Teaching, and (4) Ticket Out the Door.

● *Activity #1. Benefits and Challenges Jigsaw*

Time: 30 minutes
Materials:

Photocopy, for each participant without a book, the subsec-tion of the chapter that refers to the benefits, challenges, and cau-tions of paraprofessionals as co-teachers, so that every three people have a different benefit and a different challenge or caution as presented in the Table 8.1. For example, if there are 30 participants, then you will make 10 copies of each of the three benefits and so forth. Ask participants who have the book to read each of the subsections.

Table 8.1

Team Member A	Team Member B	Team Member C
Benefit: Inclusion and differentiation of instruction	Benefit: Cultural ambassador	Benefit: Teacher recruitment
Challenge: Poorly defined role definition	Challenge: Ambiguity in supervision responsibilities and inconsistent initial and ongoing professional development	Cautions to paraprofessionals as co-teachers

Directions:

1. This is a simple cooperative group-learning jigsaw activity. First, group participants into teams of three and assign each member a letter: A, B, or C. Then, distribute the materials as outlined in the materials section or write on the board the sections of the book each member will read.
2. Instruct the team members to read silently and prepare to teach the assigned rationale to their teammates. Suggest that they each create a visual representation of their respective content to use during their instructional time. Provide participants no more than two to three minutes to prepare.
3. Explain that the team will have two rounds of instruction. In the first round, members share what they read about benefits; in the second, they share challenges and cautions. Explain that there are three rotating roles during each round of instruction:

   Instructor/Teller—Explains the assigned rationale to teammates.

   Questioner/Clarifier—Asks clarifying questions to ensure the instructor/teller shares complete information.

   Timekeeper—Warns the instructor/teller when one minute is nearly up and signals when one minute is up.

   Explain that in the first round of instruction, member A is the first instructor/teller, member B is the first question/clarifier, and member C is the first timekeeper. These roles are rotated every *two* minutes until each member of the team has taught their section on benefits. In the second round, member B is the first instructor/teller, member C is the first question/clarifier, and member A is the first timekeeper. In this round, each member of the triad has *three* minutes to share highlights of the assigned readings on challenges and/or cautions.

4. Give members five to ten minutes to prepare their sections for instruction. Then begin the two rounds. The first round should take a total of six or seven minutes. The second round should take ten minutes or so. Close by having team members thank one another for their instruction.

● *Activity #2. Vignette Analysis*

Time: 30 minutes
Materials:

Photocopy for each participant the section titled "Meet the Paraprofessional and Her Elementary Co-Teachers" and this co-teaching team's lesson plan, presented as Resource G at the end of the book. Ask participants who have the book to read these two items.

Directions:

1. Give the participants 10 to 15 minutes to read the "Meet the Paraprofessional and Her Elementary Co-Teachers" vignette in its entirety. Give these instructions: "As you read this vignette about Ms. Katz, the paraprofessional, and her team, please put yourself in her shoes. What did the team do to ensure that she was able to perform her roles as a supportive, parallel, and complementary co-teacher? What else can you think of that would have helped you, if you were Ms. Katz?"

2. After all participants have read the vignette, assemble participants into the same triads as for the first activity and give them five or six minutes to discuss two questions: What did the team do to ensure that she was able to perform her roles as a supportive, parallel, and complementary co-teacher? What else can you think of that would have helped you, if you were Ms. Katz?

3. Debrief by sampling some of the participants' ideas about what else would have helped Ms. Katz to be successful as a paraprofessional in so many different co-teaching roles.

● *Activity #3. The Role of the Paraprofessional in Co-Teaching*

Video/DVD Activity
Time: 20–30 minutes
Materials:

Video/DVD segment titled "The Role of Paraprofessionals in Co-Teaching"
Video player with TV monitor and/or DVD player

Directions:

1. Prepare participants to watch the video/DVD segment titled "The Role of Paraprofessionals in Co-Teaching" by saying the following: "Listen and watch a paraprofessional in an elementary classroom as she explains how she promotes independence of all learners while also supporting the teachers. Notice how she does not work only with the child with a disability. In addition, see her create learning materials on the spot so that learners are better able to understand the task. Listen to her and the other co-teachers as they identify benefits and challenges of and cautions for paraprofessionals serving as co-teachers."
2. Play the video/DVD. When the video/DVD segment ends, ask participants the following series of questions:
   a. What does the paraprofessional featured in this segment describe as her greatest challenge?
   b. What does she describe as the benefits of inclusive education?
   c. What cautions do the two co-teachers interviewed offer with regard to co-teaching with paraprofessionals?
   d. What benefits do they identify in having paraprofessionals co-teach?

● *Activity #4. Ticket Out the Door*

Time: 5 minutes
Materials:

3" × 5" note cards for each participant

Directions:

1. Tell participants that their "ticket out the door" is to write on a 3" × 5" note card the answer to the following questions:
   a. What information described in Chapter 8 is most important to you?
   b. What do you need to work most effectively with a paraprofessional?
2. Allow two or three minutes for participants to complete the cards.

3. Collect the cards as "tickets" out the door. If you reconvene to study Chapter 9 or any other chapter, you can summarize their responses as part of the opening of the next workshop session.

Chapter 9: The Role of Students as Co-Teachers

The Role of Students

- Vignettes Showing Students as Co-Teachers
- Analyzing the Cooperative Process for Students as Co-Teachers
- FAQs About the Role of Students as Co-Teachers
- Preparing Students to Be Co-Teachers
- The Research Base for Students as Co-Teachers

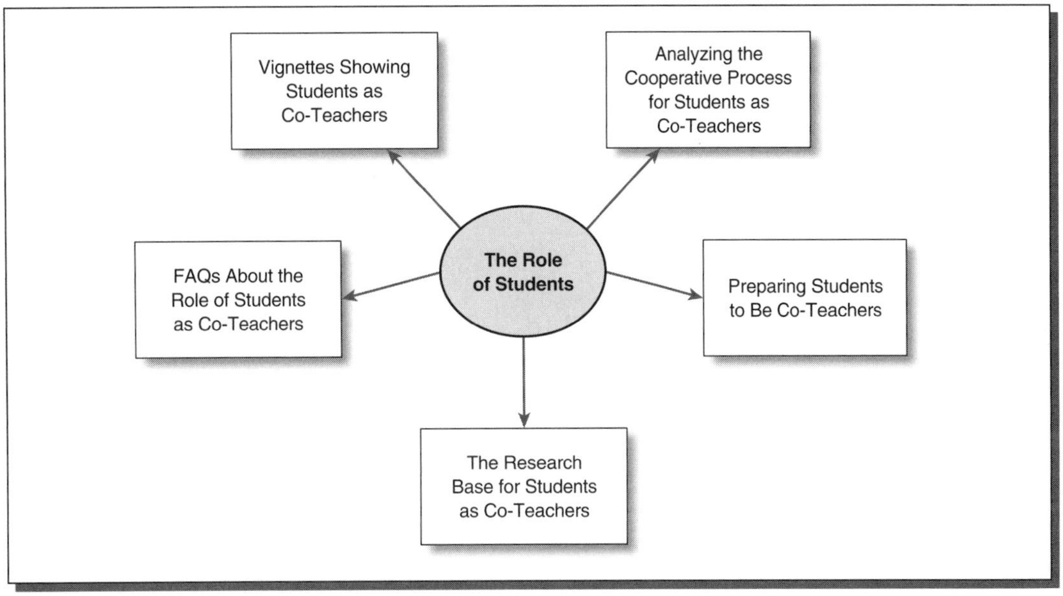

Figure 9.1   Content Map for Chapter 9

Summary

The authors define teaching in such a way that it is feasible to consider students as *co-teachers*, by emphasizing the broadest possible interpretation of that word, where teaching is the act of helping someone else to learn something. They argue that children and youth who learn how to co-teach are more likely to grow into adults who can effectively self-advocate and work as a member of a team. Several examples of children and teens and their teachers co-teaching various curricula help the reader understand the range of roles that can be shaped. To help consolidate the message that students can become effective co-teachers, the authors analyze the examples by finding the five elements of the cooperative process in action (face-to-face interaction, positive interdependence, interpersonal skills, monitoring, and accountability).

The teacher's roles and responsibilities for preparing students to be co-teachers include the following:

- Give explicit instruction on how to tutor or work as a study buddy.
- Ensure reciprocity of being both a teacher and a learner.

- Set up cooperative group lessons so that each group member can practice communication skills needed to teach others what we know.
- Teach the social skills needed to negotiate conflict (e.g., friendly disagreeing).
- Encourage students to become coaches and encouragers.
- Shift the teacher's role from presenter of information to facilitator of learning.

The authors highlight specific practices, such as dialogue teaching and instructional conversation, which help students learn to become co-teachers. They also summarize the benefits of peer tutoring and cooperative group learning strategies. For this chapter, the two frequently asked questions focus on the maturity level needed for a student to be a co-teacher and how to justify taking time from teaching the curriculum to teach the communication and collaborative skills needed to be a student co-teacher.

Discussion Questions

Decide what you would say in response to the following questions. You may work alone by responding in a personal journal, or you may discuss your answers with a partner or teammates in a small group.

1. What are three benefits to you and your students when they learn to be effective co-teachers?
2. What are your favorite ways to prepare students to be peer tutors, members of cooperative groups, or study buddies? Compare your responses with the recommendations offered by the authors for preparing students to be co-teachers.

Practical Applications

1. Interview a student co-teacher with whom you have worked. Decide how to answer each of the items on the checklist titled "Are You Really a Student Co-Teacher?" (shown in Table 9.3 in the book). Celebrate each yes. Talk through one of the items marked no to determine what you each need to do to turn it into a yes. Schedule the next meeting to celebrate the successful implementation of the ideas you generated together!
2. Observe a co-teaching lesson where students are working in co-teaching roles and subsequently listen as they reflect on the lesson.
3. Choose one of the articles that the authors list in this chapter that discusses the research evidence for students in co-teaching

roles. Read the article and discuss it with another teacher interested in students as co-teachers. What connections can you make between what is stated in the article and your own school situation?

4. Engage the students in your class with Activity #2, Meet the Student Co-Teacher Teams, described in the next section. (Note that the readability of the material given the students should be appropriate for most middle school and high school students.)

Activities for Workshop Facilitators and Course Instructors

There are four activities to help participants learn the content of Chapter 9: (1) Student Collaboration Quiz, (2) Meet the Student Co-Teacher Teams, (3) Video/DVD Activity—The Role of Students as Co-Teachers, and (4) Read and Ponder Extension Activity.

● *Activity #1. Student Collaboration Quiz*

Time: 5 minutes
Materials:

Photocopy of the Student Collaboration Quiz (Handout 9) for each participant.

Directions:

1. Have the participants visualize being back in elementary, middle, and high school and recollect their schooling experiences.
2. Hand out the Student Collaboration Quiz and instruct them to rate their overall kindergarten through grade 12 experiences using the 14 questions. Tell them you realize there were differences among their elementary, middle, and high school experiences, so their ratings will be an average of those experiences. When participants have finished, have them turn to a neighbor and share their overall results.
3. After a minute or two, reconvene the entire group, saying, "Raise your hand if you gave yourself mostly Very Often ratings." Notice that few, if any, participants will raise their hands. Repeat this question for the Often, Sometimes, Rarely, and Never ratings. Notice that most hands are raised for the Rarely and Never ratings.
4. Share with the entire group that the authors believe students in today's inclusive classrooms have more Often and Very Often ratings—if their teachers employ the collaborative practices included in this quiz and the student co-teaching practices described in Chapter 9.

5. Ask the participants if they agree or disagree with this statement: "Students who learn how to be co-teachers with younger or same-age peers have the chance to learn the collaborative skills needed to be successful in jobs and future education experiences; having the opportunity to be a co-teacher as a student gives that student a lifelong edge."

● *Activity #2. Meet the Student Co-Teacher Teams*

Time: 30 minutes
Materials:

Photocopy for each participant without a book a copy of the vignettes the "Students in Co-Teaching Roles" section of Chapter 9 in its entirety. Ask participants who have the book to open to this section of Chapter 9.

Directions:

1. Explain the "Say Something" quick cooperative group structure that is used in this activity: "In the 'Say Something' quick cooperative structure, partners read a passage, usually silently, and at given points, stop to say something about what they have just read. Each partner says something by making a connection or commenting on what that person learned in that section of the reading. For this activity, partners will stop four times. After reading each of the four vignettes, partners will pause and comment on what they learned about students as co-teachers in the vignette."

2. Pair up participants. Tell them that they will have three to five minutes to read and then say something about each of the four student co-teaching vignettes.
   - Read through the first vignette, "Bill and Sharon." After reading the vignette, each partner says something (no more than one minute collectively).
   - Read through the second vignette, "Christine and Cat." After reading the vignette, each partner says something (no more than one minute collectively).
   - Read through the third vignette, "Dave and Juan." After reading the vignette, each partner says something (no more than one minute collectively).
   - Read through the fourth vignette, "Denny, Cathy, and Shamonique." After reading the vignette, each partner says something (no more than one minute collectively).

3. Monitor the group and move them along to the next vignette when you see that pairs have read the passage and shared using the "Say Something" strategy. When they have completed all four of the vignettes, thank them for saying something. If time permits,

debrief by asking participants to share what they learned from the four vignettes about how to engage students as co-teachers.

● *Activity #3. The Role of Students as Co-Teachers*

Video/DVD Activity
Time: 20 minutes
Materials:

Video/DVD segment titled "The Role of Students as Co-Teachers"

Video player with TV monitor and/or DVD player

Photocopy Table 9.3 Checklist, "Are You Really a Student Co-Teacher?" for each participant without a book. Ask participants who have the book to open to Table 9.3.

Directions:

1. Tell participants that they will see students in various co-teaching roles described in the book, such as peer buddy and peer tutor. The video/DVD segment includes students at the elementary, middle, and high school levels. Ask them to detect which co-teaching roles the students are using and speculate what the students' teachers did to prepare them for their roles.
2. Play "The Role of Students as Co-Teachers" video/DVD segment.
3. When the segment is complete, ask participants to describe the student co-teaching roles they observed. Ask them what they thought the students' teachers did to prepare them to engage in their co-teaching roles.
4. Next, ask participants to think of two ways they might structure their own lessons so that students can learn and practice co-teaching. Have them share these ideas with a neighbor. Ask two or three participants to share their examples with the whole group.
5. Provide closure by handing out the copies of the "Are You Really a Student Co-Teacher?" checklist. Tell participants this checklist includes skills that student co-teachers need to know how to perform. This checklist can help teachers know what to teach their students so that students can better support classmates when they work as tutors, learning partners, study buddies, or cooperative group members.

● *Activity #4. Read and Ponder Extension Activity*

For participants who want to learn more about students as co-teachers, suggest that they read the sections of Chapter 9 that describe how to prepare students to be co-teachers and the research base that shows the effectiveness of students as co-teachers.

Part IV: Administrative Support and Professional Development

Chapter 10: Training and Logistical Administrative Support for Co-Teaching

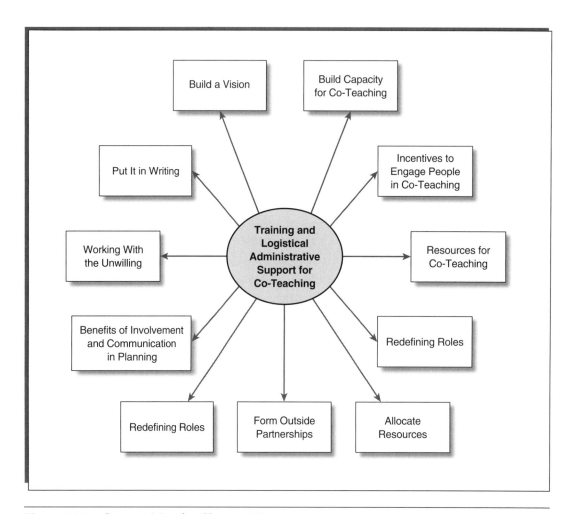

Figure 10.1 Content Map for Chapter 10

Summary

Administrators are essential catalysts who can spark an interest in and commitment to co-teaching at any school site or classroom. In this chapter, the authors provide concrete suggestions on how to (1) build support for the vision of co-teaching; (2) develop educators' skills and confidence to be co-teachers;

(3) create meaningful incentives for co-teachers; (4) reorganize, schedule, and expand human and other resources for co-teaching; and (5) plan for and take action designed to motivate teachers and administrators to implement co-teaching in a school. Throughout the chapter, the authors emphasize ways schools can restructure to make co-teaching a part of the normal day-to-day operation of a school. When administrators ensure that all five elements of complex change (vision, skills, incentives, resources, action plan) are addressed in the ways described in this chapter, the result can be a remarkable increase in a school's capacity for co-teaching.

Discussion Questions

Decide what you would say in response to the following questions. You may work alone by responding in a personal journal, or you may discuss your answers with a partner or teammates in a small group.

1. In the "Building a Vision" section of Chapter 10, the authors write, "Simply stating a vision (for co-teaching) is not enough." In your opinion, what more is needed to build a *vision*? In other words, what are your ideas on how to build a vision? How do your ideas compare to the authors' suggestions for building a vision?
2. In your opinion, what *skills* are important for teachers and other professional and paraprofessional staff to acquire to be effective in using co-teaching as a way to increase student success?
3. What *incentives* and *resources* do you believe would motivate the teachers you know to use the four co-teaching approaches? Which factors are motivators for you? Compare your suggestions with the incentives and resources described in Chapter 10.
4. Which elements of complex change—vision, skills, incentives, resources, and action planning—are being considered and addressed in your school to promote a systems change to co-teaching? Using the "Action Plan Template" (Resource K in the book), identify the actions you would take to build consensus for a vision of co-teaching, to develop skills, to create incentives, and to mobilize or redistribute resources. Feel free to use the sample one-year action plan (text Figure 10.1) included in the chapter as a model for completing your own action plan.

Practical Applications

1. Volunteer to work on a planning committee to implement some aspect of co-teaching in your school. Keep a journal of your experiences and notice the impact of (1) establishing a team vision, (2) building team consensus toward achieving one goal, (3) structuring incentives for yourself and your committee teammates, (4) finding and allocating resources to achieve the goal (e.g., finding an outside-of-school partner), and (5) creating an action plan (such as the "Sample Action Plan" in text Figure 10.1) to present to a leadership representative or governing body (e.g., superintendent, building principal, or school PTA president).

2. Decide to implement the Vision + Skills + Incentives + Resources + Action Plan complex change formula with your students to achieve a class goal (e.g., a class field trip, a service-learning project, a fundraising event, a design for a play, or a songfest to share with other classes). Keep a journal of the experience.

3. Share your knowledge and experiences by explaining the Vision + Skills + Incentives + Resources + Action Plan complex change process with someone else.

Activities for Workshop Facilitators and Course Instructors

There are three activities to help participants learn the content of Chapter 10: (1) Cooperative Jigsaw of Vision + Skills + Incentives + Resources + Action Plan Complex Change Process, (2) Video/DVD Activity—Training and Logistical Administrative Support for Co-Teaching, and (3) Frequently Asked Questions.

● *Activity #1. Cooperative Jigsaw of Vision + Skills + Incentives + Resources + Action Plan Complex Change Process*

In this activity, participants are grouped interdependently so that each member of the group teaches a section of the Vision + Skills + Incentives + Resources + Action Plan Secret for Systems Change and Goal Achievement.

Time: 40–45 minutes
Materials:

Photocopy for each participant without a book each of the five sections of Chapter 10, so each team member has the assigned section of the chapter. If there are 20 participants, there will be four groups of 5 and, therefore, a need for four sets of copies of the chapter sections that address the 5 elements (vision, skills, incentives, resources, action plan) of the complex change formula. Ask participants who have the book to open to the relevant section.

Directions:

1. Organize the participants into study groups with four members each. Tell the participants that each member of the study group will be responsible for reading, summarizing, and reporting various aspects of the "secret formula" for successful school restructuring to achieve co-teaching in their school. Assign each member of the group a letter: *A, B, C,* or *D.*
   - *A*s will read, summarize, and teach study group members the "Building a Vision" content.
   - *B*s will read, summarize, and teach study group members the "Building the Skills and Capacity for Co-Teaching" and "Incentives to Engage People in Co-Teaching" content.
   - *C*s will read, summarize, and teach study group members the "Resources for Co-Teaching" content.
   - *D*s will read, summarize, and teach study group members the "Getting Started: Planning and Taking Action" content.
2. Ask each group member to study for approximately 20 minutes, then to summarize and prepare to teach their sections of the complex change formula. Encourage the participants to create visual representations of their elements of the formula. Also, tell them that each team member has no more than four minutes to teach the element(s).
3. After 20 minutes, set the teams into motion by having the *A* member begin instruction of how to promote a vision. The *B* member is the timekeeper, who provides a one-minute warning and stops the teaching at the four-minute limit. Rotate instruction, so the *B* member now teaches and the *C* member is the timekeeper. Repeat this with the *C* member being the teacher and the *D* member being the timekeeper. Finish with member *D* teaching and member *A* timekeeping.
4. Monitor the groups as they jigsaw teach to be sure the members abide by the time limits. After 15 to 20 minutes of the jigsaw instruction, stop the teamwork and ask team members to thank their study group partners for their instruction.
5. Reconvene the entire group to debrief what participants learned. Select one *A*, one *B*, one *C*, and one *D* to share their reactions to the material, listening carefully for concerns and/or questions. If there is time, open the session to the entire group for sharing of outcomes and examples of each of the five elements in action in a change initiative with which a participant may have been involved.

● *Activity #2. Training and Logistical Administrative Support for Co-Teaching*

Video/DVD Activity
Time: 20–30 minutes
Materials:

Handout 10: Note-Taking Guide: Complex Change

Video/DVD segment titled "Training and Logistical Administrative Support for Co-Teaching"

Video player with TV monitor and/or DVD player

Directions:

1. Direct participants to observe carefully and take notes as they listen to Dr. Villa and school administrators, teachers, and paraprofessionals talk about administrative supports they have experienced. Tell participants that each interviewee's comment falls into one or more of the five categories of the complex change process: vision, skills, incentives, resources, and action plan. Say, "As you watch the interviews, please use the Complex Change Note-Taking Form to categorize their comments."
2. Play the video/DVD segment, "Training and Logistical Administrative Support for Co-Teaching."
3. Debrief the video/DVD viewing by first asking, "What did you hear the interviewees say about how to promote vision, skills, incentives, resources, and action plans for co-teaching?" Sample some responses from the participants for each of the five elements.

● *Activity #3. Frequently Asked Questions*

Time: 10–15 minutes
Materials:

Photocopy "Frequently Asked Questions" from Chapter 10 for each participant without a book. Ask participants who have the book to open to the "Frequently Asked Questions" section of Chapter 10.

Directions:

1. Turn to "Frequently Asked Questions" at the end of Chapter 10. Do not read the answers to the questions. Instead, read each question and compose your own answer. If you are working with a group, rotate the role of reader for each of the questions.
2. Compare your answers to each question, then read the response written in the text. In what ways were your responses similar or different? What new ideas did you get from the authors' response to each question?

Chapter 11: Meshing Planning With Co-Teaching

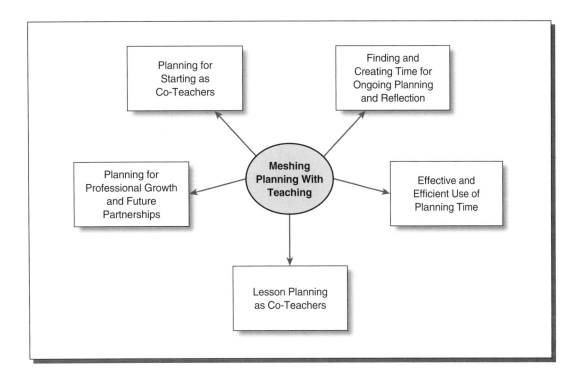

Figure 11.1 Content Map for Chapter 11

Summary

This is a content-rich chapter that helps readers plan their journey as co-teachers. The authors offer suggestions for finding or creating time for planning and reflection. They introduce a "Co-Teaching Planning Meeting Agenda Format," which co-teachers can use to make co-teaching planning meetings more effective and efficient. The authors introduce the "Suggested Co-Teaching Daily Lesson Plan Format," which helps co-teachers engage systematically in the recursive planning-analysis-reflection format for co-taught lessons. The detailed questions and cues listed in the lesson plan template allow co-teachers to think about the essential elements of any good lesson plan. Because the lesson plan is for two or more co-teachers, three additional questions prompt co-teachers to deliberately consider (1) which of the four types of co-teaching arrangements the team will use; (2) exactly what each individual co-teacher will be doing before, during, and after the lesson; and (3) how the room will be arranged so that each co-teacher has the needed space to deliver instruction. The chapter ends with a 34-item self-assessment checklist titled "Are We Really Co-Teachers?" The checklist is a tool for co-teachers to identify key co-teaching actions and to rate their current performance to set goals for professional development.

Discussion Questions

Decide what you would say in response to the following questions. You may work alone by responding in a personal journal, or you may discuss your answers with a partner or teammates in a small group.

1. Please examine the strategies for expanding time for planning presented in Table 11.1 in the book. Which of these strategies are the most appealing to you and why? Which would be most appealing to your co-teaching colleagues or school administrators and why?
2. Please examine the "Co-Teaching Planning Meeting Agenda Format," presented as Resource L at the end of the book. Without looking at the text in the book, identify where on the lesson plan the cooperative process element of *face-to-face interaction* is prompted. Where is *positive interdependence* structured into the agenda? How does the agenda hold co-teachers accountable for completing the tasks to which they commit? What in the agenda ensures future face-to-face interaction?
3. Please examine the "Are We Really Co-Teachers?" self-assessment checklist, presented as Resource M at the end of the book. In what ways might the items on this checklist help you, a reflective practitioner, become a more effective co-teaching team member?

Practical Applications

1. Think of a curriculum or teaching task you must accomplish that requires you to convene a meeting. Use the "Co-Teaching Planning Meeting Agenda Format," presented as Resource L at the end of the book, to manage the meeting. Reflect upon the meeting by asking yourself the following: How did the format help you to accomplish your agenda items? How did it help you to move the agenda along in a timely fashion? How did it assist in clarifying tasks and responsibilities to be carried out after the meeting?"
2. Practice developing a co-taught lesson using the "Suggested Co-Teacher Lesson Plan Format," presented in the book as Resource L or in this guide as Handout 11: Co-Teaching Daily Lesson Plan Template. See also Table 11.2 in the book, which shows how an elementary co-teaching team used the agenda to structure a planning meeting. Was the format detailed enough for you and

your co-teacher to be clear on your roles before, during, and after the lesson? Is there anything you would add or change?

3. Handout 12: Tips and Strategies for Role Differentiation—Teacher Actions During Co-Teaching, provides many concrete suggestions of how co-teachers can differentiate and coordinate their actions during a supportive, parallel, complementary, or team-teaching lesson. Please study these examples and decide which of the co-teaching approaches each represents.

4. Please use Handout 13: Tips and Strategies for Role Differentiation—Co-Teacher Actions During Lessons (Blank), to brainstorm ways in which to differentiate your role with your current or prospective co-teaching partner. Also, identify which of the four co-teaching approaches—supportive, parallel, complementary, or team-teaching—your division of labor represents. Because this tool is a good conversation starter about the differentiation of co-teaching roles, try using it with each of your new co-teaching partners to help them think of ideas about ways in which you might try each of the four co-teaching approaches.

5. There is a saying, "We know what is respected by what is expected and inspected." Knowing the importance of having a professional development tool for inspecting practice that matches what is expected, consider using Handout 14: Co-Teaching Instructional Observation Form. This form was designed by a school administrator specifically to empower co-teachers and their professional coaches and supervisors to assess and reflect upon how they use the co-teaching approaches, as well as various ways they differentiate instruction through co-teaching. For this application, you may choose to ask someone to use the form to observe you and your co-teaching partner as you implement a co-taught lesson. You may want to use the form yourself to observe others as they co-teach. You may choose to observe a paraprofessional whom you supervise or another co-teaching team that you are coaching. After using the observation form, reflect on how effective it was in helping you to clarify what was going on in the classroom to facilitate student learning through co-teaching.

6. Think of different ways you can assess yourself as you work with one of your co-teaching teams. Invite your co-teachers to choose one of the self-assessment systems listed in Handout 15: Co-Teaching Self-Monitoring Systems.

Activities for Workshop Facilitators and Course Instructors

The activities that follow may be used in two ways. As with the previous chapters, you can choose to present the activities consecutively, one at a time. Alternately, the participants can attend stations, or centers, in a parallel, station-teaching instructional arrangement. In this arrangement, participants can rotate from one station to another, selecting among the stations the ones that are of most interest to them. Station teaching encourages participants to partner with others who have similar interests. It also allows you to show rather than tell how important it is, and how easy it is, to differentiate instruction according to the interests of the participants.

● *Preparing for Center/Station Teaching*

For the station-teaching option, you can introduce the experience by setting up the room into distinct areas, where the materials needed for each of the station activities are arranged. Chart paper or colorful posters with a clearly marked station name and clearly summarized directions should be placed over the station area and table holding the station materials. This alerts participants to the focus of each of the stations and ensures that participants know what to do when they get there.

You can begin the session by saying, "Chapter 11 provides many practical tools and strategies for meshing planning with co-teaching. Today we will use the station-teaching approach to show rather than tell how the tools included in this chapter help co-teachers to prepare better to teach and reflect upon their instruction. You notice that six centers, or stations, are set up around this room."

Briefly describe each station and tell participants that the activity at each station takes approximately ten minutes to complete. If you have 65 to 70 minutes for this training session, then have participants rotate to all six stations. If you have less time, ask them to rotate to as many stations as they can in the time limit. If you have only 25 to 30 minutes for the training session, including setting up the session with these instructions: participants can choose among two stations. If you have 35 to 40 minutes, they can choose three; if you have 45 to 50 minutes, they can choose four; if you have 50 to 55 minutes, they can choose five.

● *The Centers or Stations*

The six center, or station, activities for Chapter 11 are the following:

STATION I: If One Does This, The Other Can Do . . .
STATION II: Finding and Creating Time to Plan

STATION III: Building an Agenda

STATION IV: Lesson Planning for Co-Teachers

STATION V: Are We Really a Co-Teaching Team?

STATION VI: Video/DVD Activity—Meshing Planning With Teaching

● *Monitoring Station Activities*

Allow about ten minutes per learning station and circulate to each station to listen as participants engage in the activities or to clarify expectations. Two minutes before the time limit, say, "In two minutes, your group will move clockwise to the next learning station. Please complete your thoughts, thank your partners, gather your belongings and your notes from this learning station, and get ready to move." At the ten-minute mark, signal the participants to move to another station.

● *Closure*

The facilitator reconvenes the entire group to debrief by asking participants to write down three things they learned about meshing planning with co-teaching from the stations they attended. Have participants share with a neighbor and then sample the answers from four or five participants. Thank the participants for their cooperation in working together during the station-teaching experience.

● *Activity #1. If One Does This, The Other Can Do . . .*

Time: 10 minutes
Materials:

Photocopies of the following handouts for all participants:

Handout 12: Tips and Strategies for Role Differentiation—Teacher Actions During Co-Teaching

Handout 13: Tips and Strategies for Role Differentiation—Co-Teacher Actions During Lessons (Blank)

Directions:

1. Find a partner or two, preferably someone with whom you are or might be co-teaching. Examine Handout 12: Tips and Strategies for Role Differentiation—Teacher Actions During Co-Teaching, which provides many concrete suggestions of how co-teachers can differentiate and coordinate their actions during a supportive, parallel, complementary, or team-teaching lesson.

2. Now pick up Handout 13: Tips and Strategies for Role Differentiation—Co-Teacher Actions During Lessons (Blank), and practice differentiating your co-teaching roles. This worksheet provides space for you to differentiate your role with a co-teacher. With your partner(s), brainstorm, as prompted in the worksheet, ways in which "If one of you is doing this . . . the other can be doing this . . ." Also, identify which of the four co-teaching approaches—supportive, parallel, complementary, or team-teaching—your division of labor represents.

3. Extension activity: Because this tool is a good conversation starter about the differentiation of co-teacher roles, try this exercise anytime you have a new or prospective co-teaching partner to help you think of ways you might differentiate roles for each of the four co-teaching approaches.

● *Activity #2. Finding and Creating Time to Plan*

Time: 10 minutes
Materials:

Photocopy for each participant Table 11.1, Strategies for Expanding Time for Planning, from of the book.

Highlighter markers for each participant

Directions:

1. Find a partner or two. Someone you co-teach with would be a good partner.

2. With your partner(s), systematically examine the 17 strategies for expanding time for planning. As you read through them, identify which strategies you already have in place. Using the markers, highlight the strategies that you consider to be the most supportive, appealing, and doable—ones you might advocate for with your administrator and/or co-teacher(s).

● *Activity #3. Building an Agenda*

Time: 10 minutes
Materials:

Photocopy for each participant the "Co-Teaching Planning Meeting Agenda Format" (Resource L at the end of the book).

Highlighter markers for each participant

Directions:

1. Find a partner(s). You should each have a copy of the "Co-Teaching Planning Meeting Agenda Format." Study the elements. If you are with someone who is a co-teacher or who attends one or more common meetings with you, examine the agenda together.
2. Think of a curriculum or teaching task you must accomplish that requires you to convene a meeting. Use the "Co-Teaching Planning Meeting Agenda Format" to plan the meeting.
3. Compare your meeting agenda with that of another team and discuss the following questions: What were the differences in roles for those who attended the meeting? What differences did you notice in terms of agenda items or time limits? What differences did you notice in terms of building the agenda for the next meeting?
4. Extension activity: Use the agenda you planned during this activity to manage the meeting. Reflect upon the meeting. How did the format help you to accomplish your agenda items? How did it help you to move the agenda along in a timely fashion? How did it assist in clarifying tasks and responsibilities to be carried out after the meeting?

● *Activity #4. Lesson Planning for Co-Teachers*

Time: 10 minutes
Materials:

Several copies of *A Guide to Co-Teaching: Practical Tips for Facilitating Student Learning*, 2nd edition, for participants to flip through and examine the sample lesson plans shown as Resources C through H, or several photocopies of these lessons

Handout 11: Co-Teaching Daily Lesson Plan Template—one for each participant

Directions:

1. Briefly review examples of the co-teaching lessons described in Chapters 4, 5, 6, 7, 8, and 9 and the corresponding lesson plans presented as Resources C through H in the book.
2. With another person who has similar interests or grade level assignment, draft a co-teaching lesson using Handout 11: Co-Teaching Daily Lesson Plan Template.
3. As you are drafting the lesson, consider the following questions about the lesson plan template: Was the format detailed enough for you and your co-teacher to be clear on your roles before,

during, and after the lesson? Is there anything you would add or change?

4. If there is time (i.e., if you are doing this activity as a stand-alone activity and you have 20 or 30 minutes), share or exchange your lessons with another team and review one another's lesson plans. Provide authentic feedback to enhance each other's work. Remember to praise as well as make constructive suggestions!

● *Activity #5. Are We Really Co-Teachers?*

Time: 10 minutes
Materials:

Photocopy for each participant Resource M, the "Are We Really Co-Teachers?" self-assessment checklist, from the book.

Directions:

1. Determine the current reality of one or more of your own co-teaching teams by completing the "Are We Really Co-Teachers?" checklist. If you co-teach with another participant, please do the checklist together. Set two or three goals based on what you discover.

2. Feel free to repeat this team self-assessment for another co-teaching team, if you are on more than one team.

● *Activity #6. Meshing Planning With Teaching*

Video/DVD Activity
Time: 10 minutes
Materials:

Computer for the video/DVD segment titled "Meshing Planning with Teaching"

Directions:

1. Play the segment titled "Meshing Planning with Teaching." Please take notes on what co-teachers are saying about meshing planning with teaching. The video/DVD segment is about eight minutes long.

2. After the video/DVD segment is complete, discuss with your teammates what you learned, or what was reinforced that you already knew, with regard to meshing planning with teaching.

Chapter 12: From Surviving to Thriving: Tips for Getting Along With Your Co-Teachers

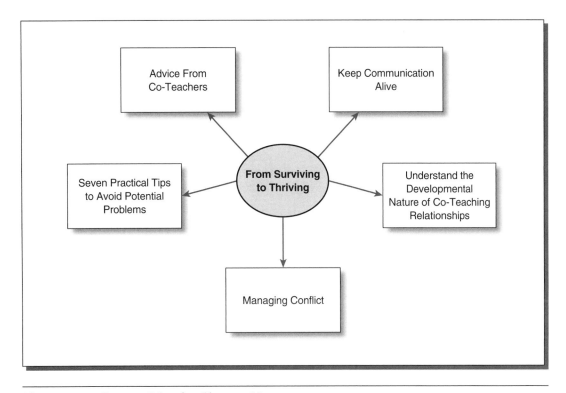

Figure 12.1   Content Map for Chapter 12

Summary

What do you need to thrive in a co-teaching situation? In this chapter, the authors share several strategies and frameworks for addressing challenges that have helped other co-teachers learn to appreciate and work with a wide variety of co-teacher partners, including those whom they at first experienced as resistant or even hostile to the idea of co-teaching. Communication skills, psychological supports, and problem-solving strategies are detailed with examples. Co-teacher relationships follow developmental stages similar to the stages of development that children experience. Practical tips to handle challenging or unproductive behavior are described, as well as tips to avoid potential problems.

Discussion Questions

Decide what you would say in response to the following questions. You may work alone by responding in a personal journal, or you may discuss your answers with a partner or teammates in a small group.

1. Why do you think the authors suggest that learning how to co-teach is a developmental process? What have you noticed about others' comfort with and development of the skills needed to be an effective collaborator? What have you noticed about your own comfort with and development of the skills needed to be an effective collaborator?

2. In the section "Managing Conflict," the authors suggest that conflict is natural and that there is research to support the idea that conflict has value. Do you agree or disagree with these assertions? Why?

3. Read the sections titled "Managing Conflict" and "Tips for Dealing With Challenging and Unproductive Behavior." What is your opinion of the contention that conflict (and constructive confrontation of unproductive behavior) can be valuable to a team? Write down and/or discuss your rationale with another teacher.

Practical Applications

1. In Table 12.4 in the book, the authors list eight tips to help co-teachers avoid potential conflicts. Select two that you are especially interested in learning how to do. Keep a journal of your experiences as you practice those tips and notice the changes in your relationships with other teaching partners.

2. When planning and debriefing lessons, co-teachers can be more effective if they use some of the roles suggested in this chapter. Try using at least one of the roles in the book's Table 12.2 that facilitates goal achievement and one of the roles in Table 12.3 that maintains interpersonal relationships. Select roles that you think really will help you in your meetings. For example, if one of the team members often puts down ideas before they can be developed, it might be wise to select the "Yes, but . . ." monitor role that is used to signal (and stop) judgments being made during brainstorming.

3. The next time you experience a team member's engaging in challenging or unproductive behavior, use the five-step procedure for confronting a person outlined in the "Tips for Dealing With Challenging and Unproductive Behavior" sections of Chapter 12. How well did you follow the steps? How did the person respond? What can you do to improve your skill in using this method for dealing with conflict?

4. Are there any tips that the authors did not include? Share your own tips with two other participants and ask them what their tips are.

Activities for Workshop Facilitators and Course Instructors

There are two activities to help participants learn the information in this chapter: (1) Poster Gallery Walk (for Practical Tips to Avoid

Potential Problems) and (2) Video/DVD Activity—Tips for Teachers.

● *Activity #1. Poster Gallery Walk*
  (for Practical Tips to Avoid Potential Problems)

Time: 30–40 minutes
Materials:

Four pieces of large poster paper and masking tape or tacks to hang the posters

Sets of four differently colored markers

Advance Preparation
There are four poster stations for this gallery walk. Four of the eight tips for avoiding potential problems among co-teachers are featured on this walk: Tips 1, 3, 4, and 5. Post the paper around the room in advance. Write the tip number and the tip itself at the top of the first poster paper

Tip 1. Know with whom you need to co-teach.

Tip 3. Agree to use a common conceptual framework, language, and set of interpersonal skills.

Tip 4. Practice communication skills for successful co-teacher interactions—achieving the tasks and maintaining positive relationships.

Tip 5. Know how to facilitate a collaborative culture.

Directions:

1. Invite participants to form four groups based upon any criteria (e.g., random, school, age group of students taught, similar subject, or birth month).
2. Each group is given a differently colored marker and stationed at one of the four posters. Directions for each of the stations are presented below and posted at the stations. Have the participants read the instructions and then engage in the task at their station.
3. At the designated time (usually no more than four or five minutes), move each group clockwise to the next poster. Remind them to bring their markers with them. Tell them to read the instructions for the station as well as what the previous team has written. They are to add their own items in their own color. One member of the group will act as recorder to scribe until the facilitator signals to switch recorders and move to the next poster.

4. Repeat Step 3 until each group has been to each of the four stations.
5. Closure: Thank the participants for sharing how they avoid potential problems among co-teachers, then invite them to wander around the "gallery" to admire their works/words of art.

● *Gallery Station Tip #1. Know with whom you need to co-teach.*

Materials:

Hang four sheets of chart paper side-by-side. Label the two on the left, "Roles of others with whom I may co-teach." Label the two on the right, "Expertise this person has that my students or I need/could benefit from."

Directions:

Hang an instruction page in large font that states the following steps:

1. Think of all of the people with whom you could co-teach.
2. List their roles on the left.
3. For each of these people, what are some of the gifts and talents they can bring to your students and to you? Please list these on the right.
4. Be sure each member of your group has contributed at least one name and noted some of that person's gifts.

● *Gallery Station Tip #3. Agree to use a common conceptual framework, language, and set of interpersonal skills.*

Materials:

Hang four sheets of chart paper side-by-side. Label the two on the left "Ground rules or norms" Label the two on the right "Strategies to promote the following of this ground rule."

Copy and hang on the wall above these sheets Table 12.1, A Checklist of Skills for the Stages of Co-Teacher Development.

Directions:

Hang an instruction page in large font that states the following:

1. All teams must agree upon norms or ground rules to help them function. Think of some ground rules that are important to you. For instance, arriving at meetings on time is an important norm

for many people. So one ground rule would be "We arrive to meetings on time."

2. Your task is to formulate a few important norms and record them on the left-hand chart paper.

3. Record on the right-hand chart paper at least one strategy for enforcing this norm. Table 12.1 may help you to formulate some norms. In our example, one strategy to promote the norm of "We arrive to meetings on time" is to write in the minutes of the meeting those who are present and those who are not when the meeting starts.

● *Gallery Station Tip #4. Practice communication skills for successful co-teacher interactions.*

Materials:

Hang four sheets of chart paper side-by-side. Photocopy and tape Table 12.2, Roles for Co-Teachers: Roles That Facilitate Goal Achievement, above the two pieces of chart paper on the left. Photocopy and tape Table 12.3, Roles That Maintain Positive Interpersonal Relationships, above the two pieces of chart paper on the right.

Directions:

Hang an instruction page in large font that states the following:

1. When planning and debriefing lessons, co-teachers can be more effective if they use some of the roles posted on the chart papers to the left and right.

2. The chart papers on the left, from Table 12.2, facilitate goal achievement.

3. The chart papers on the right, from Table 12.3, help maintain interpersonal relationships.

4. Take a look at the nine roles. Invent a role to help get the task done that you can name and define it on the left-hand poster. Invent another role that builds relationships. Name and define it on the right-hand chart paper.

● *Gallery Station Tip #5. Know how to facilitate a collaborative culture.*

Materials:

Hang five sheets of chart paper side-by-side, each with a different label from Glasser's basic human needs: survival, power or control in one's life, freedom of choice, a sense of belonging, and fun.

Directions:
Hang an instruction page in large font that states the following:

1. The motivational theorist William Glasser suggests that we all have the five needs listed on these five pieces of chart paper.
2. Your task is to invent ways to facilitate a collaborative culture by helping one another meet the five needs as teachers. What can you do as co-teachers and colleagues to help one another survive, have some power and choice, create a sense of community, and have some fun? Have fun generating and recording ideas in each of the five categories!

● *Activity #2. Tips for Teachers*

Video/DVD Activity
Time: 20 minutes
Materials:

Handout 16: Tips for Co-Teachers to Avoid Potential Problems

Video/DVD segment titled "From Surviving to Thriving: Tips for Getting Along With Your Co-Teachers"

Video player with TV monitor and/or DVD player

Directions:

1. Distribute Handout 16: Tips for Co-Teachers to Avoid Potential Problems. Briefly, tell participants that this video/DVD segment shows teachers, paraprofessionals, and administrators offering tips for a co-teacher. Ask them to keep in mind the tips listed on the handout as they listen to the advice given on the video.
2. Play the video/DVD segment titled "From Surviving to Thriving: Tips for Getting Along With Your Co-Teachers."
3. When the video/DVD segment is complete, ask, "What did you hear? Compare the advice from these people with the list of tips to avoid potential problems. Discuss your ideas with a partner."
4. Then ask, "Based upon the advice from the co-teachers, paraprofessionals, and administrators in the video, what additional tips would you add?" Sample a few responses from participants for this and the previous questions.
5. Compare your notes about what the interviewees advised with the list on Handout 16. What is similar? What is different?
6. After five to six minutes of sharing, reconvene the entire group. The facilitator asks three or four participants to share ideas with the larger group.

Epilogue: Developing a Shared Voice Through Co-Teaching

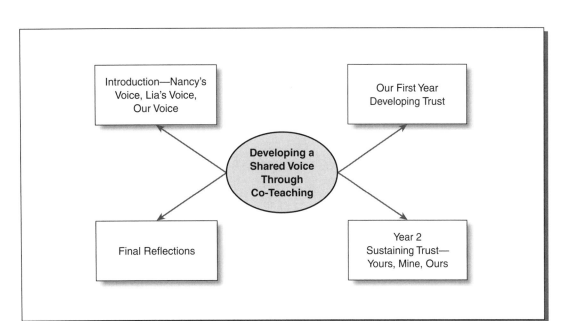

Figure E.1   Content Map for Epilogue

Summary

What happens when a science teacher collaborates with a special educator so their students with disabilities, who are being included in the general education classroom, would benefit as much as possible? How Nancy (the science teacher) and Lia (the special educator) collaborated and what happened to each of them is the content for this epilogue. Throughout the co-teachers' journey, readers learn how the co-teachers practiced one or more of the eight tips to avoid potential conflicts and problems. During the first year, Nancy and Lia focused on their communication skills to develop trust. In the second year, they emphasized the skills for sustaining trust. (For a review of the stages of group development and the skills needed at each stage, see Chapter 12 and Resource N.) As you read Nancy and Lia's story in their voices, you begin to appreciate the differences in the way each has been prepared as a professional educator. As they become accustomed to one another's frame of reference, a blended voice emerges. The co-teachers describe how they implemented the elements of the cooperative planning process (i.e., how they structured face-to-face planning time, established positive interdependence by clarifying their respective roles, ensured individual accountability, and monitored and debriefed along the way). You also hear them speak about how they improved their own teaching skills by learning from one another's strengths.

Discussion Questions

Decide what you would say in response to the following questions. You may work alone by responding in a personal journal, or you may discuss your answers with a partner or others in a small group.

1. Why might a co-teaching approach be a foreign way of thinking at first about planning and implementing instruction?
2. What "spoke to you?" What could you identify with in Nancy and/or Lia's voice as they talked about their two-year co-teaching journey?
3. As a result of learning about co-teaching, what new assumptions and beliefs have you acquired? How have your assumptions or beliefs been changed or affirmed?

Practical Applications

1. Create and display a scrapbook, drawing, mobile, collage, or cartoon strip to illustrate your assumptions and beliefs about co-teaching.
2. Given Nancy and Lia's illustrations of the eight tips for avoiding problems between co-teachers, come up with your own strategies for each of the eight tips and record them on a copy of Handout 16: Tips for Co-Teachers to Avoid Potential Problems, worksheet.

Activities for Workshop Facilitators and Course Instructors

There are two activities designed to help participants understand the content of this epilogue: (1) Readers Theater Plus (Ratliff, 1999) and (2) The Report Card.

● *Activity #1. Readers Theater Plus*

Time: 20–40 minutes
Directions for Part 1:

1. Ask two participants to be the voices of Nancy and Lia. Give them about three minutes to scan the sections titled "Nancy's Voice" and "Lia's Voice," then ask Nancy to read first.

2. Explain this activity to the participants by saying, "First, we'll listen to Nancy's voice, then to Lia's voice. Next, we'll listen as both Nancy and Lia read "Our Voice' together." Alternate paragraph by paragraph: Nancy reads the first and third paragraphs; Lia reads the second and fourth paragraphs. "As the listener, you can either read along or just listen."

3. When "Nancy" and "Lia" are finished speaking, ask participants to turn to a neighbor and share an impression or reflection of what they heard while listening to the voices of this co-teacher team.

Directions for Part 2:

1. Have participants find partners and invite them to read silently the section titled "Our First Year—Developing Trust."

2. Tell them to pause and talk periodically to exchange comments by using the quick cooperative "Say Something" technique. For this retrospective's "Say Something" exercise, partners will pause at the end of each of the subsections of the Year 1 text and each say something about the text that relates to the topic or shared voice of the tip being emphasized.

Directions for Part 3:

1. Repeat the steps of Part 2 for the "Year 2—Sustaining Trust" pages of Nancy and Lia's experiences.

2. Complete this Readers Theater Plus activity by reading "Final Reflections" and talking about how Nancy and Lia accomplished Tip 6, recognizing and respecting differences and multiple sources of motivation.

● *Activity #2. The Report Card*

Time: 5 minutes
Materials:

Photocopy for each participant of Handout 17: Blank "Report Card"

Directions:

1. Analyze what you learned from Nancy and Lia's account of developing a shared voice through co-teaching in terms of their development from striving to thriving over their two-year co-teaching journey. Practice giving positive feedback to others

by using the "Dear colleague" Report Card template. Write a letter to Nancy and Lia.

2. Ask yourself, "If I received a letter like this, how would I feel?" Then role-play giving Nancy or Lia the letter by exchanging it with another participant.

3. Read the letter you receive and, with your partner, discuss how it felt to write and receive the Report Card letter and how you might express what you learn from others in even better ways.

Workshop Evaluation and Closure

The purpose of this activity is to provide a formal process to complete the workshop and to collect participants' evaluations of the workshop. The authors and Corwin Press will gratefully acknowledge the facilitators who gather this information, which will provide valuable feedback for the next edition of the material.

Time: 10–15 minutes
Materials:

Workshop Evaluation Form

Directions:

1. Distribute a copy of the Workshop Evaluation Form, provided in the *Facilitator Guide,* to each participant.
2. Ask participants to be honest as they respond to each item.
3. Explain that the evaluation form is sent to Corwin Press Speaker's Bureau for collating, summarizing, and returning to the workshop facilitator.
4. Explain that thorough feedback is helpful in guiding redesign of future workshops.
5. After ten minutes, ask how many participants need more time. If possible, extend the time another five minutes.
6. Ask participants who have completed the evaluation form to hand it to the session organizer (*not* the workshop facilitator). Explain again that the evaluations will be collated and sent to the authors and the publisher (Corwin Press) and will provide valuable feedback for future editions.
7. Thank the participants for their willingness to provide meaningful feedback and say good-bye.

Workshop Evaluation Form

How well did the workshop meet its goal and objectives?

How will you apply what you learned during this workshop in your daily professional life?

What professional support will you need to implement what you have learned from this workshop?

How well did the topics explored in this workshop meet a specific need in your school or district?

How relevant was this topic to your professional life?

Process

How well did the instructional techniques and activities facilitate your understanding of the topic?

How can you incorporate the activities learned today into your daily professional life?

Were a variety of learning experiences included in the workshop?

Was any particular activity memorable? What made it stand out?

Context

Were the facilities conducive to learning?

Were the accommodations adequate for the activities involved?

Overall

Overall, how successful would you consider this workshop? Please include a brief comment or explanation.

What was the most valuable thing you gained from this workshop experience?

Additional Comments

Source: Adapted from *Evaluating Professional Development* by Thomas R. Guskey, Corwin Press, 2000.

Overheads and Handouts

Handout 1. Definition of Co-Teaching

Co-teaching is . . .

- two or more people sharing responsibility for teaching some or all of the students assigned to one classroom.

- a fun way for students to learn from two or more people who have different ways of thinking or teaching.

- a creative way to support and connect with others and to help all children learn.

- a way to make schools more effective.

And co-teaching is like a marriage because . . .

- it's not always 50/50.

- it takes time to develop a relationship.

- there will be differences.

- you may need a marriage counselor (consultant) from time to time.

Handout 2. Five Elements of the Cooperative Process for Co-Teachers: Note-Taking Guide

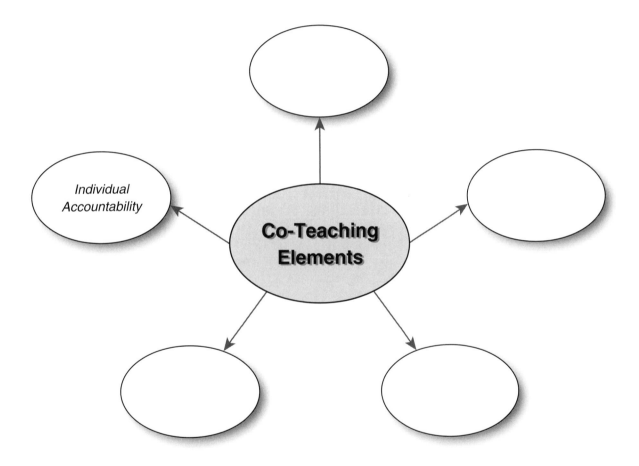

Handout 3. What Co-Teaching Is and Is Not

Co-Teaching Is . . .	Co-Teaching Is Not . . .

Handout 4. Note-Taking Guide for Video/DVD of Chapter 2: Why Co-Teach?

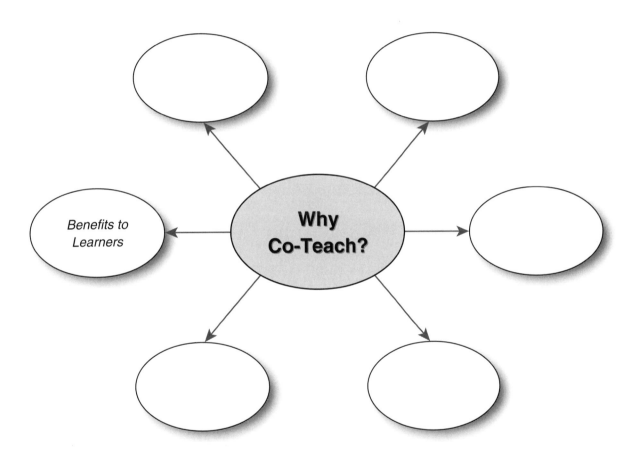

Handout 5. Advance Organizer: Issues for Discussion

Directions: Individually brainstorm, then discuss with a partner or small group, how you would address the following issues that co-teachers need to address. Make sure you write down at least one idea for each issue. If you think of other issues, add them.

Time for Planning

●
●
●

Instruction

●
●
●

Managing Discipline (Student Behavior)

●
●
●

Communication

●
●
●

Evaluation

●
●
●

Logistics

●
●
●

Other?

●
●
●

Handout 6. Definitions of Co-Teaching Approaches

Supportive co-teaching is when one educator takes the lead and other educators rotate among students to provide support.

Parallel co-teaching is when co-teachers instruct different heterogeneous groups of students.

Complementary co-teaching is when a co-teacher does something to supplement or complement the instruction provided by the educator (e.g., models note-taking on a transparency or paraphrases the teacher's statements).

Team teaching co-teaching is when co-teachers share and distribute among themselves the responsibility for planning, teaching, and assessing the progress of all students in the class.

Handout 7. Similarities and Differences of Supportive, Parallel, Complementary, and Team-Teaching Co-Teaching Approaches

Similarities Among the Four Co-Teaching Approaches

Supportive Differences	*Parallel Differences*	*Complementary Differences*	*Team-Teaching Differences*
Supportive Cautions	*Parallel Cautions*	*Complementary Cautions*	*Team-Teaching Cautions*

Handout 8. SODAS Problem-Solving Process

SITUATION (Define the problem):

_____

_____

OPTIONS:

1._____   2. _____   3. _____

DISADVANTAGES:

a. _____   a. _____   a. _____

b. _____   b. _____   b. _____

c. _____   c. _____   c. _____

d._____   d. _____   d. _____

ADVANTAGES:

a. _____   a. _____   a. _____

b. _____   b. _____   b. _____

c. _____   c. _____   c. _____

d._____   d. _____   d. _____

SOLUTION:

_If_ you agree to a solution, make a plan.
(Who will do what, and when? How will you know if the plan is working?)

Handout 9. Student Collaboration Quiz

1. When you were a student, did you observe or experience your teachers modeling collaboration in instruction (team teaching), planning, or evaluation?

   Never   Rarely   Sometimes   Often   Very Often

2. Were you, as a student, given the opportunity and coaching to serve as an instructor for a peer?

   Never   Rarely   Sometimes   Often   Very Often

3. Were you, as a student, given the opportunity to receive instruction from a trained peer?

   Never   Rarely   Sometimes   Often   Very Often

4. How often was the instruction you received structured in such a way as to encourage the use of higher-level reasoning skills (e.g., analysis, synthesis, evaluation, creative problem solving, or meta-cognition)?

   Never   Rarely   Sometimes   Often   Very Often

5. How often were you expected to support the academic and social learning of other students, as well as be accountable for your own learning?

   Never   Rarely   Sometimes   Often   Very Often

6. Were you, as a student, given the opportunity and training to serve as a mediator of conflict between peers?

   Never   Rarely   Sometimes   Often   Very Often

7. How often were you asked to evaluate your own learning?

   Never   Rarely   Sometimes   Often   Very Often

8. How often were you given the opportunity to assist in determining the educational outcome for you and your classmates?

   Never   Rarely   Sometimes   Often   Very Often

9. How often were you given the opportunity to advocate for the educational interests of a classmate or asked to assist in determining modifications and accommodations to curriculum?

Never   Rarely   Sometimes   Often   Very Often

10. How often were you, as a student, encouraged to bring a support person to a difficult meeting to provide you with moral support?

Never   Rarely   Sometimes   Often   Very Often

11. How often were you involved in a discussion of the teaching with an instructor?

Never   Rarely   Sometimes   Often   Very Often

12. How often were you asked to provide your teachers with feedback as to the effectiveness and appropriateness of their instruction and classroom management?

Never   Rarely   Sometimes   Often   Very Often

13. How often did you participate as an equal with teachers, administrators, and community members on school committees (e.g., curriculum committee, discipline committee, hiring committee, or school board)?

Never   Rarely   Sometimes   Often   Very Often

14. How often did you, as a student, feel that the school "belonged" to you—that school experiences were structured primarily with student interests in mind?

Never   Rarely   Sometimes   Often   Very Often

Handout 10. Note-Taking Guide: Complex Change

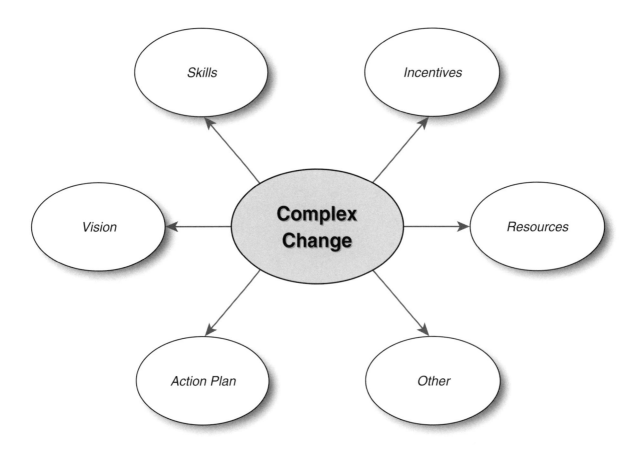

Handout 11. Co-Teaching Daily Lesson Plan Template

Date: _____ Co-Teachers: _____

Content Area(s): _____ Roles: _____

Lesson Objectives:

Content Standards Addressed:

Circle the Co-Teaching Model(s) Used: Supportive   Parallel   Complementary   Team Teaching

What is the room arrangement? Will spaces outside of the classroom be used? (Draw a picture of the room arrangement.)

What materials do the co-teachers need?

How is student learning assessed by co-teachers?

What specific supports, aids, or services do select students need? (See Resource A in *A Guide to Co-Teaching: Practical Tips for Facilitating Student Learning*, 2nd Edition for suggestions.)

What does each co-teacher do before, during, and after the lesson?

Co-Teacher Name:				
What are the specific tasks that I do before the lesson?				
What are the specific tasks that I do during the lesson?				
What are the specific tasks that I do after the lesson?				

Reflection: Where, when, and how do co-teachers debrief and evaluate the outcomes of the lesson?

Handout 12. Tips and Strategies for Role Differentiation—Teacher Actions During Co-Teaching

If one of you is doing this . . .	*The other can be doing this . . .*
Lecturing	Modeling note-taking on the board/overhead
Taking roll	Collecting and/or reviewing last night's homework
Passing out papers	Reviewing directions
Giving instructions orally	Writing down instructions on board
Checking for understanding with large, heterogeneous group of students	Checking for understanding with small, heterogeneous group of students
Providing direct instruction to whole class	Circulating, providing one-on-one support as needed
Prepping half of the class for one side of a debate	Prepping the other half of the class for the opposing side of the debate
Facilitating a silent activity	Circulating, checking for comprehension
Providing large-group instruction	Circulating, using proximity control for behavior management
Running last-minute copies or errands	Reviewing homework
Reteaching or preteaching with a small group	Monitoring large group as they work on practice materials
Facilitating sustained silent reading	Reading aloud quietly with a small group; previewing upcoming information
Reading a test aloud to a group of students	Proctoring a test silently with a group of students
Creating basic lesson plans for standards, objective, and content curriculum	Providing suggestions for modifications, accommodations, and activities for diverse learners
Facilitating stations or groups	Facilitating other stations or groups
Explaining new concept	Conducting a role-play or modeling the concept
Considering modification needs	Considering enrichment opportunities

Murawski, W., & Dieker, L. (2004). Tips and strategies for co-teaching at the secondary level. *Teaching Exceptional Children, 36*(5), 53–58. Shared with permission.

Handout 13. Tips and Strategies for Role Differentiation—Co-Teacher Actions During Lessons (Blank)

If one of you is doing this . . .	The other can be doing this . . .	Co-Teaching Approach
Providing direct instruction to whole class	Circulating, providing one-on-one support as needed	Supportive
Giving instructions orally	Writing down instructions on board	Complementary
Guiding students through odd steps of a procedure	Guiding students through even steps of a procedure	Team Teaching
Prepping half of the class for one side of a debate	Prepping the other half of the class for the opposing side of the debate	Parallel

Handout 14. Co-Teacher Instructional Observation Form

Use this form as part of a professional development program to provide authentic feedback and coaching as co-teachers develop their skills.

Teacher(s):	Observer:	Date:	Class Period/Time Frame:
Grade Level(s):	Subject Area(s):	Scheduled Observation: ☐ Yes	Drop-in Observation: ☐ Yes

Co-Teaching Approach(es)

Supportive: ☐ Yes ☐ No _____

Parallel: ☐ Yes ☐ No _____

Complementary: ☐ Yes ☐ No _____

Team Teaching: ☐ Yes ☐ No _____

Students as Co-Teachers: ☐ Yes ☐ No _____

Instructional Arrangements

Cooperative learning structures: ☐ Yes ☐ No _____

Same or cross-age peer tutors: ☐ Yes ☐ No _____

Independent: ☐ Yes ☐ No _____

Whole group: ☐ Yes ☐ No _____

Tutorial: ☐ Yes ☐ No _____

Teacher- or paraprofessional-directed small group: ☐ Yes ☐ No _____

Social and Physical Environment

Room arrangement adapted: ☐ Yes ☐ No _____

Spaces used outside of class: ☐ Yes ☐ No _____

Clear and evident routines: ☐ Yes ☐ No _____

Directions given clearly: ☐ Yes ☐ No _____

Positive behavioral supports: ☐ Yes ☐ No _____

Transition times are smooth: ☐ Yes ☐ No _____

Next Steps

Written feedback: ☐ Yes ☐ No _____

Instructional observation: ☐ Yes ☐ No _____

Coaching cycle: ☐ Yes ☐ No _____

Conference/debrief: ☐ Yes ☐ No _____

District training: ☐ Yes ☐ No _____

Other: _____

Additional Notes

Adapted from Wiseman, 2006.

Handout 15. Co-Teaching Self-Monitoring Systems

Name of System and Description	Focus and Rationale
Co-Teacher Relationship Scale— A tool for matching potential members of co-teaching teams, developed by Noonan, McCormick, & Heck (2003). This is a self-rating scale that allows ratings on two dimensions, one of beliefs and attitudes about teaching and classroom management and the other of philosophies that underlie the teaching method. Co-teachers rate the extent to which they agree or disagree with each other.	Focus: attitudes, beliefs, and personal characteristics of co-teachers Rationale: Can help co-teachers see how they change their attitudes, beliefs, and actions as they learn from each other. May help match potential co-teaching team members, depending on the extent to which they agree on select items.
Are We Really a Co-Teacher Team? Survey— A tool to improve co-teaching actions. Developed by Villa, Thousand, & Nevin (2008). On this self-assessment survey, co-teachers answer yes or no, depending on if they both agree that they do the actions or behaviors described in 35 items.	Focus: teacher actions and behaviors Rationale: Can use the results as a diagnostic tool to design professional development activities. Can be used to set goals for enhancing how co-teacher team members work together. May help administrators design specific professional development activities.
Co-Teacher Quality Indicators Model— This useful tool for guiding improvement of co-teaching actions developed by Magiera & Simmons (2005) for use as a self- or administrator assessment scale includes examples and definitions of the sequential skills that observers can see effective co-teachers use (including professionalism, classroom management, instructional process, grouping, and monitoring student progress).	Focus: examples and definitions of sequential skills co-teachers need Rationale: Can be an alternative evaluation procedure, which co-teachers can ask their supervisors to use. Can be used to guide co-teacher professional development activities.

Handout 16. Tips for Co-Teachers to Avoid Potential Problems

Tip 1: Know with whom you need to co-teach.
Tip 2: Establish and clarify co-teaching goals to avoid hidden agendas.
Tip 3: Agree to use a common conceptual framework, language, and set of interpersonal skills.
Tip 4: Practice communication skills for successful co-teacher interactions so you can achieve goals and maintain positive relationships.
Tip 5: Know how to facilitate a collaborative culture.
Tip 6: Recognize and respect differences in excellence and the multiple sources of motivation for co-teaching.
Tip 7: Expect to be responsible and expect to be held accountable.
Tip 8: Agree to reflective analysis of co-teaching lessons and celebrate often.
Other tips?

Handout 17. The Report Card (Blank)

Name of Co-Teachers:

Some things I learned from observing you are . . .

(Examples: How you find time to plan and reflect, how you are accountable for student achievement, how you share responsibilities and roles, . . .)

Something you might do differently in your next lesson is . . .

Signed: _____   Date: _____

Matrix of Activities and Estimated Times

Title	Activity	Estimated Time	Cumulative TOTAL
Welcome and Workshop Starter	Activity #1. Workshop Introduction Activity Activity #2. Cocktail Party Activity	10–15 minutes 15 minutes	30 minutes
PART I			
Chapter 1	Activity #1. Cooperative Group Learning Jigsaw—Five Elements of the Cooperative Process Activity #2. Video/DVD Activity—What Co-Teaching Is and Is Not	10 minutes 30 minutes	70 minutes (1 hour 10 minutes)
Chapter 2	Activity #1. Summary and Guided Practice Jigsaw Activity #2. Video/DVD Activity—Why Co-Teach?	20–30 minutes 10 minutes	110 minutes (1 hour 50 minutes)
Chapter 3	Activity #1. Issues to Discuss Activity #2. Video/DVD Activity—The Day-to-Day Workings of Co-Teaching Teams	10 minutes 30 minutes	150 minutes (2 hours 30 minutes)
PART II	Activity #1. Compare and Contrast the Co-Teaching Approaches	25 minutes	175 minutes (2 hours 55 minutes)
Chapter 4	Activity #1. Read and Apply Activity #2. Video/DVD Activity—The Supportive Co-Teaching Approach Activity #3. Frequently Asked Questions and Cautions	5–10 minutes 20–30 minutes 15 minutes	230 minutes (3 hours 50 minutes)
Chapter 5	Activity #1. Read and Apply Activity #2. The Many Faces of Parallel Co-Teaching Activity #3. Video/DVD Activity—The Parallel Co-Teaching Approach Activity #4. Frequently Asked Questions and Cautions	5–10 minutes 10 minutes 20–30 minutes 10–15 minutes	295 minutes (4 hours 55 minutes)

(Continued)

(Continued)

Title	Activity	Estimated Time	Cumulative TOTAL
Chapter 6	Activity #1. Read and Apply Activity #2. Video/DVD Activity—The Complementary Co-Teaching Approach Activity #3. Frequently Asked Questions and Cautions	5–10 minutes 20–30 minutes 10–15 minutes	350 minutes (5 hours 50 minutes)
Chapter 7	Activity #1. Read and Apply Activity #2. Video/DVD Activity—The Team-Teaching Co-Teaching Approach Activity #3. Frequently Asked Questions and Cautions Integration Activity #1. Compare and Contrast the Four Approaches to Co-Teaching Integration Activity #2. Dance Co-Teaching Integration Activity #3. Video/DVD Activity—Steven and Stephanie—Compare and Contrast Team Teaching With Other Co-Teaching Approaches	5–10 minutes 20–30 minutes 25–30 minutes 20 minutes 10–15 minutes 15 minutes	470 minutes (7 hours 50 minutes)
PART III			
Chapter 8	Activity #1. Benefits and Challenges Jigsaw Activity #2. Vignette Analysis Activity #3. Video/DVD Activity—The Role of the Paraprofessional in Co-Teaching Activity #4. Ticket Out the Door	30 minutes 30 minutes 20–30 minutes 5 minutes	565 minutes (9 hours 25 minutes)
Chapter 9	Activity #1. Student Collaboration Quiz Activity #2. Meet the Student Co-Teacher Teams	5 minutes 30 minutes	620 minutes (10 hours 20 minutes)

	Activity #3. Video/DVD Activity—The Role of Students as Co-Teachers	20 minutes	
	Activity #4. Read and Ponder Extension Activity	—	
PART IV			
Chapter 10	Activity #1. Cooperative Jigsaw of Vision + Skills + Incentives + Resources + Action Plan Complex Change Process	40–45 minutes	710 minutes (11 hours 50 minutes)
	Activity #2. Video/DVD Activity—Training and Logistical Administrative Support for Co-Teaching	20–30 minutes	
	Activity #3. Frequently Asked Questions	10–15 minutes	
Chapter 11	Activity #1. If One Does This, The Other Can Do . . .	10 minutes	770 minutes (12 hours 50 minutes)
	Activity #2. Finding and Creating Time to Plan	10 minutes	
	Activity #3. Building an Agenda	10 minutes	
	Activity #4. Lesson Planning for Co-Teachers	10 minutes	
	Activity #5. Are We Really Co-Teachers?	10 minutes	
	Activity #6. Meshing Planning With Teaching	10 minutes	
Chapter 12	Activity #1. Poster Gallery Walk (for Practical Tips to Avoid Potential Problems)	30–40 minutes	830 minutes (13 hours 50 minutes)
	Activity #2. Video/DVD Activity—Tips for Teachers	20 minutes	
Epilogue	Activity #1. Readers Theater Plus	20–40 minutes	875 minutes (14 hours 35 minutes)
	Activity #2. The Report Card	5 minutes	
Workshop Evaluation	Workshop Evaluation Activity	10–15 minutes	890 minutes (14 hours 50 minutes) [~15 hours total time]

*Note to Facilitators: Use the matrix to construct agendas for workshops of various lengths (e.g., half-day workshop (3 hours); one-day workshop (6 hours); two- or three-day workshop (6–8 hours); or 15-week course format, typically requiring a total 45 hours of instruction for a university credit-generating course).

Notes

References

Anderson, L., & Krathwohl, D. (Eds.). (2001). *A taxonomy for learning, teaching, and assessing: A revision of Bloom's taxonomy of educational objectives.* New York: Longman.

Council for Exceptional Children (CEC). (2003). *What every special educator must know: CEC international standards for entry into professional practice* (5th ed.). Arlington, VA: Author. Retrieved November 7, 2007, from www.cec.sped.org/Content/NavigationMenu/ProfessionalDevelopment/ProfessionalStandards/Red_book_5th_edition.pdf

Cramer, E., & Nevin, A. (2006). A mixed methodology analysis of co-teacher assessments: Implications for teacher education. *Teacher Education and Special Education, 29*(4), 261–274.

Cramer, E., Nevin, A., Thousand, J., & Liston, A. (2006, January). *Co-teaching in urban school districts to meet the needs of all teachers and learners: Implications for teacher education reform.* Refereed paper presented at American Association of Colleges for Teacher Education, San Diego, CA. (ERIC Document Reproduction Service No. ED491651)

Friend, M. (2008). *Co-teach! A manual for creating and sustaining effective classroom partnerships in inclusive schools.* Greensboro, NC: Author.

Giordano, V. (2005, April). A professional development model to promote Internet integration in K–12 teaching practices. In M. Cleary, M. Plakhotnik, & S. Nielsen (Eds.), *Proceedings of the fifth annual college of education research conference* (pp. 48–54). Miami: Florida International University, College of Education.

Hall, G. E., & Hord, S. M. (2001). *Implementing change: Patterns, principles, and potholes.* Needham Heights, MA: Allyn and Bacon.

Hall, T. 2002. *Differentiated instruction.* Wakefield, MA: National Center on Accessing the General Curriculum. Retrieved November 7, 2007, from www.cast.org/publications/ncac/ncac_diffinstruc.html

Hord, S. M. (1992). *Facilitative leadership: The imperative for change.* Austin, TX: Southwest Educational Development Laboratory.

Interstate New Teacher Assessment and Support Consortium (INTASC). (2006). *Interstate new teacher assessment and support consortium standards.* Washington, DC: Council of Chief State Schools Officers. Retrieved November 7, 2007, from www.ccsso.org/projects/Interstate_New_Teacher_Assessment_and_Support_Consortium/

Liston, A. (2006, April). Evaluation of the status of a co-teacher instructional delivery approach in urban and multicultural secondary education settings. Unpublished dissertation, Argosy University, Orange, CA.

Magiera, K. A., & Simmons, R. J. (2005). *Guidebook for the Magiera-Simmons quality indicator model of co-teaching.* Fredonia, NY: Excelsior Educational Service.

Marzano, R., Pickering, D., & Pollock, J. (2001). *Classroom instruction that works: Research-based strategies for increasing student achievement.* Alexandria, VA: Association for Supervision and Curriculum Development.

National Board Professional Teaching Standards (NBPTS). (2006). *Performance-based teaching assessments.* Princeton, NJ: Educational Testing Services.

Noonan, M., McCormick, L., & Heck, R. (2003). The co-teacher relationship scale: Applications for professional development. *Education and Training in Developmental Disabilities, 38*(1), 113–120.

Ratliff, G. (1999). *Introduction to readers theatre: A guide to classroom performance.* Colorado Springs, CO: Meriwether Publishing.

Roy, P. (2005, February). A fresh look at follow-up. National Staff Development Council *Results.* Retrieved November 7, 2007, from www.nsdc.org/library/publications/results/res2-05roy.cfm

Schultz, L. (2005). *Bloom's taxonomy.* Retrieved November 7, 2007, from Old Dominion University Web site: www.odu.edu/educ/llschult/blooms_taxonomy.htm

Starr, L. (2004). Strategy of the week: Differentiated instruction. *Education World.* Retrieved November 7, 2007, from www.educationworld.com/a_curr/strategy/strategy042.shtml

Thousand, J. S., Villa, R. A., & Nevin, A. I. (2007). *Differentiating instruction: Collaborative planning and teaching for universally designed learning.* Thousand Oaks, CA: Corwin Press.

Villa, R. A., Thousand, J. S., & Nevin, A. I. (2008). *A guide to co-teaching: Practical tips for facilitating student learning* (2nd ed.). Thousand Oaks, CA: Corwin Press.

Willis, S., & Mann, L. (2000, Winter). Differentiating instruction: Finding manageable ways to meet individual needs. Association for Supervision and Curriculum Development *Curriculum Update.* Retrieved November 7, 2007, from www.ascd.org/ed_topics/cu2000win_willis.html

Wiseman, J. (2006, Fall). *Lesson Plan Evaluation Form.* San Diego Unified School District.

**CORWIN
PRESS**

The Corwin Press logo—a raven striding across an open book—represents the union of courage and learning. Corwin Press is committed to improving education for all learners by publishing books and other professional development resources for those serving the field of PreK–12 education. By providing practical, hands-on materials, Corwin Press continues to carry out the promise of its motto: **"Helping Educators Do Their Work Better."**

The worldwide mission of The Council for Exceptional Children is to improve educational outcomes for individuals with exceptionalities.

CEC, a non-profit association, accomplishes its mission, which is carried out in support of special education professionals and others working on behalf of individuals with exceptionalities, by advocating for appropriate governmental policies, by setting professional standards, by providing continuing professional development, by advocating for newly and historically underserved individuals with exceptionalities, and by helping professionals achieve the conditions and resources necessary for effective professional practice.